AN
OCEAN
OF
FLAVOR

ALSO BY ELIZABETH ANDOH

At Home with Japanese Cooking
(*Knopf, 1980*)

An American Taste of Japan
(*Morrow, 1985*)

AN OCEAN OF FLAVOR

The Japanese Way with Fish and Seafood

Elizabeth Andoh

Illustrated by Isabel Samaras

WILLIAM MORROW AND COMPANY, INC.

NEW YORK

Some recipes were originally printed, in different form, in the following publications:

Spicy Skewered Shrimp, Glaze-Grilled Swordfish, and Snapper Grilled with Fragrant Pepper originally appeared in *Food & Wine* magazine in May 1986.

Crunchy Fried Shrimp originally appeared in *Bon Appétit* magazine in January 1982.

Broth with Squid and Vegetables and Hot-Stone Fish Stew appeared in *Gourmet* magazine in 1988.

Library of Congress Cataloging-in-Publication Data

Andoh, Elizabeth.
  An ocean of flavor.

  Includes index.
    1. Cookery (Seafood) 2. Cookery, Japanese.
I. Title.
TX747.A624 1988   641.6'92   88-12741
ISBN 0-688-07061-2

Printed in the United States of America

First Edition

1 2 3 4 5 6 7 8 9 10

BOOK DESIGN BY KATHIE PARISE

Acknowledgments

Many people were generous in sharing their time, knowledge and talent with me. I am enormously grateful for their help.

I want to thank my editor at William Morrow, Maria Guarnaschelli, for her inspiration, enthusiasm, and editorial vision. In addition, I am indebted to my talented illustrator, Isabel Samaras; jacket designer, Gloria Adelson; and book designers Maria Epes, and Kathryn Parise, for the visual appeal of this book. My literary agent, Molly Friedrich, helped smooth the way over occasional rough moments, and Maria's assistant, Julia Kent, was also helpful in many little, but important, ways.

My dear friend Eiko Ohta and the women of the Andoh family—particularly my mother-in-law, Kiyoko Andoh, and sisters-in-law, Yohko Yokoi and Nobuko Okashita—first introduced me to the wonders of Japanese home cooking and continue to share their love of good food with me. The Yanagihara family, both Master Toshio and his son Master Kazunari, had the patience and courage to educate me in the ways of the traditional professional Japanese kitchen. My formal studies at the Yanagihara school began in 1969, and I am just now beginning to understand how much there is for me to learn.

Over the years, my husband, Atsunori, and our daughter,

Acknowledgments

Rena, have been my most severe critics and loyal fans. Their comments and suggestions continue to be invaluable. My mother, Caroline Saxe, has also been of tremendous help in both listening to ideas and tasting a variety of foods. I was ably and cheerfully assisted in testing recipes for this book by Lori Longbotham, Anna Brandenburger, Suzanne Waugh, and Joanna Bergman.

Finally, I trully appreciate those fellow food professionals and members of the seafood industry who have answered my many questions. In Charleston, South Carolina: Donna Florio, Dr. Michael L. Jahncke, Robert H. Dunlap, Jr., and William H. Lacy III. In Seattle, Washington, and Vancouver, British Columbia: Beverly Gruber, John Doerper, Mauny Kaseburg, Jon Rowley, and Sinclair Philip.

Contents

Contents

A Note About the Romanization and Pronunciation of the Japanese Language

There is a great deal of controversy and confusion over the best means of transcribing the Japanese language into the Roman alphabet. For the American cook and restaurant-goer who wants to buy Japanese ingredients and understand a menu, the lack of uniformity is very frustrating indeed.

In this book I have chosen to follow the well-known and respected Hepburn system for spelling, since it makes the most sense to speakers of standard American English. The Hepburn system includes the macron, or "long mark," over certain vowels that are meant to be extended in sound. This macron is useful in distinguishing between words that would otherwise be spelled the same: *ōba* is a broad-leafed herb, *oba* is an aunt.

Since no official system provides a visual clue to the correct pronunciation of the letter "e" (which sounds like "ay"), I have borrowed a familiar symbol from the French. That way, seeing an accent mark above the "e," Americans will know that *agé* must be pronounced "ah-gay," not "age."

In Japanese all "g" sounds are hard, as in "good" or "great"; soft "g" sounds are written with a "j."

Written Japanese is a steady flow of symbols rarely broken by spaces between words, or even by punctuation. No official system of romanization includes guidelines on how to break Japanese words on a page. But since a lengthy string of

9

unfamiliar combinations of letters is daunting to most readers, I have decided to break Japanese titles into units of meaning. Rather than write *wakaménomisoshiru* as one impossibly long word, I've broken it into a series of four: *wakamé* (sea-tangle), *no* (a possessive article), *miso* (fermented bean paste), and *shiru* (soup or liquid). Whenever a close association of words caused a phonetic change, I've used a hyphen to create a compound word to show that special relationship. Alone, vinagered rice dishes are called *sushi*, but rolled *sushi* is called *maki-zushi* (*maki* means "to roll").

My annotated system of romanization is meant to ease any difficulty you might have in pronouncing the original Japanese. I hope you find it helpful.

Introduction

W hen I first went to Japan, more than twenty years ago, it was to study the art and culture of a land that had intrigued me. I soon discovered that reading about a country can be quite different from actually living there, particularly when it comes to such everyday concerns as housing and food. Sleeping on fluffy *futon* mattresses laid out each night on a tatami-matted floor was exotic, but comfortable. The limited hot water and lack of central heating, on the other hand, came as unpleasant surprises my first winter in Tokyo. Long underwear helped keep me warm, as did nightly soaks in the deep, nearly scalding-hot tubs the Japanese call *ofuro*. But that first year, I worried most about having to eat strange things I had never heard of or tasted before, especially when they appeared on the dormitory's cafeteria menu. As soon as the university permitted me to seek separate lodgings, I rented a room with kitchen privileges and learned how to cook.

The Ohta family, with whom I stayed, was very kind to me. Eiko Ohta and her daughter, Masumi, then three years old, patiently taught me the rudiments of a Japanese kitchen: how to cook rice and how to make *dashi* stock. Next I learned to make simple simmered and grilled dishes with lots of vegetables and fish. Friends, neighbors, shopkeepers, and later the women of the Andoh clan shared their knowledge of Japanese home cooking with me. My appetite grew, and with it a deepening appreciation of Japanese cuisine and culture that eventually led me to pursue a professional course of training at the Yanagihara School of Classical Japanese Cooking in Tokyo.

At the Yanagihara School I frst became aware of the staggering variety of fish, shellfish, and sea vegetables in the Japanese diet. I hadn't known that such tasty foods as *sayori* (a lean, sweet-tasting fish with the appearance of a diminutive · swordfish) and *mana-gatsuo* (a rich, oily fish resembling our pompano), *shijimi* (tiny jet-black freshwater clams), *kombu* (kelp for stock), and *hijiki* (a lustrous black sea vegetable with a faint anise-like taste) were there in the oceans and streams, just waiting to be savored. As I learned to transform these ingredients into classical Japanese dishes, I in turn began to share my newfound knowledge and love of Japanese cooking by teaching classes to fellow Americans living in Japan.

For many years I wrote a biweekly cooking column for an English-language paper in Tokyo, and I also began to write for several American food journals, such as *Gourmet*. My first cookbook, *At Home with Japanese Cooking*, was written to help others, like myself, who had not been brought up in a Japanese environment but still wanted to cook Japanese food in their own homes. My second cookbook, *An American Taste of Japan*, was written after my return to the United States several years ago. It celebrated the glories of cross-cultural cuisine, those marvelous mixtures of American ingredients and Japanese techniques (such as the California Roll *sushi*), and Japanese foodstuffs and Continental-style dining (like *shiitaké*-smothered lamb chops) that have recently captured the American gastronomic fancy. With this book, I have returned to the inspiration for so much of Japanese cuisine, the sea. .

The majority of the recipes make use of readily available seafood—such familiar sea creatures as salmon, flounder, shrimp, scallops, and crab—albeit prepared in unique and rather extraordinary ways. Several recipes call for more unusual sea species, such as monkfish, catfish, conch, and squid. A few additional recipes make use of appealing aquatic vegetables in soups, salads, *sushi,* and sautéed dishes.

Many of the techniques and seasonings called for in this cookbook were developed and nurtured in the traditional Japanese kitchen and are, as yet, unfamiliar to many American home cooks. I've adapted typically Japanese preparations such as ''air-drying'' and ''sea-steaming'' to the American kitchen so that you can enjoy cooking fish in tasty new ways.

The book begins with guidelines for selecting and storing fish and seafood, since shopping for quality ingredients can be confusing. Next come the recipes: soups and stocks, followed by a section devoted to just *sushi* and *sashimi,* then appetizers, main courses, and finally side dishes. ''A Peek in the Pantry'' explains all the Japanese ingredients you'll encounter in the recipe section, giving recommendations for storage as well as purchase.

I suggest that you browse through the recipes, stopping to savor what attracts your interest—an unusual name such as Hot-Stone Fish Stew might arouse your curiosity, or perhaps Cold Poached Tilefish with Mellow Mustard Sauce will sound particularly appealing on a muggy day. Whether you choose to make a sauté of land and sea vegetables to accompany a roast or an omelet, or an assemblage of fanciful Golden Purse *sushi* for a luncheon entrée, you'll find this cookbook filled with new ideas for preparing a wide variety of seafood.

The Japanese have been enjoying the bounty of their oceans, streams, and seas for thousands of years, while we have just recently become aware of the enormous food resources that our own national waterways contain. Nutritional experts are urging us to incorporate more fish and shellfish into our daily menus, and I hope that with this collection of enticing recipes inspired by Japanese culinary tradition, you will be encouraged to enjoy our nation's bountiful catch.

Going to Market: A Guide to Shopping and Storage

Guidelines for choosing top-quality shellfish and finfish, plus information on handling and storing fresh, frozen, smoked, and packaged seafood

All fish and shellfish is perishable, and if not handled properly, the quality deteriorates rapidly. Since any damage, from the time the fish is hooked or the shellfish netted, is irreversible, it's crucial to select the very best seafood and to store it well to maintain optimal quality. The following guide begins with tips for buying the best, then goes on to explain how to store finfish and shellfish, whether fresh, frozen, smoked, or packaged.

If the fish is whole, the eyes should be clear and full, with no traces of blood or cloudiness. The gills should be bright red or pink, with no sour odor. The body cavity should be clean (eviscerated), with no sign of "belly burn." ("Belly burn" is caused by the fish's own caustic digestive enzymes, which continue to "burn" through the gut wall and leak into the body cavity if a fish is caught just after it has been feeding and is not gutted immediately. Typically, this "burn" appears brownish and scarred.) The skin and scales of the fish should not be bruised and should be firm to the touch. The skin should be moist, but not slimy.

Whole fish should be rinsed in cold water, patted dry, and wrapped loosely in clean parchment or waxed paper before refrigerating. Use it within 24 hours if you will be cooking or

marinating it; within 6 hours if you will be preparing it for *sashimi*.

If the fish is filleted or in steaks, the flesh should be firm and moist, with a translucent sheen to it; there should be no gaps between segments of the flesh. The odor should be fresh, never ammonia-like. After bringing them home, rinse the fillets or steaks under cold water, pat them dry, and either cook immediately or refrigerate for up to 24 hours after wrapping them in clean parchment or waxed paper, or in plastic bags or wrap.

If the fish is frozen, there should be no signs of "freezer burn," which is caused by loss of moisture through the crystallization of the fish's natural water content. This dehydration process typically causes the fish to appear chalky, and the texture of such fish after cooking is fibrous and tough.

Thaw the fish in the refrigerator, or in a sealed plastic bag

under running cold water; thawed fish should never be refrozen. If you need to hold defrosted fish an extra day, rinse the fish under cold water, pat it dry, and place it on a clean plate. Wrap the plate snugly with clear plastic wrap and refrigerate immediately.

If the fish is smoked, it should have a bright, glossy surface with no traces of salt or blood. The texture of the flesh should be firm but silky. Usually oily fishes such as salmon and sable are the easiest to smoke well, although top-quality whole drawn (eviscerated) fishes such as trout and chubb are also readily available in the marketplace. For whole smoked fish, the skin should be moist but not sticky to the touch, and the flesh should flake away easily from the bones. Wrap smoked fish snugly in clear plastic wrap before refrigerating. Use it within 36 hours of purchase for optimal flavor and texture. Smoked salmon may be frozen (check to make sure the smoked fish hasn't been frozen previously for shipment): Lay the slices on parchment or waxed paper, and cover with another sheet of paper. Roll up the sheets jelly-roll fashion, and enclose the roll snugly in clear plastic wrap.

If the fish is canned, or packaged in vacuum-sealed pouches, the container should not be punctured, leaking, or bulging in any manner. Any visible liquid should not be foamy. Canned tuna and salmon are packed in either oil or water; the choice of which to buy is one of personal taste. Usually oil-packed fish is richer and more flavorful, but water-packed fish has far fewer calories. Once a can or package has been opened, transfer the remaining contents to a covered, airtight, non-metal container and refrigerate. Use within 36 hours.

Shrimp heads should be firmly attached to the tail section. The flesh should be firm and translucent, free of black spots. Color varies with the species from gray to blue to pink (all shrimp when cooked in their shells will turn red). The odor should be fresh and mild, never ammonia-like.

FRESH
SHELLFISH

19

Transfer the shrimp to a clean plate and cover loosely with parchment or waxed paper or plastic wrap. For optimum quality, set your covered plate of shrimp over a bowl of ice. Use fresh shrimp within 24 hours of purchase; refrigerate until ready to use.

Live lobster and crabs ideally should still be swimming in oxygenated tanks, plucked from the water when you buy them; they should be lively while in the tanks. Occasionally, live lobsters and crabs will be displayed on beds of shaved ice.

If this is the case, check the eyes for clarity and the shell for uniformity of color. Poke the creature to test reflexes, which should be lively. Lobsters and crabs vary in color according to species; some are primarily brown, others more blue or green, and still others quite red even before cooking (all varieties of lobster and crab turn orangy red after cooking).

Wrap loosely and store in the warmest section (probably the vegetable bin) of your refrigerator to prevent suffocation until ready to use. Use within 12 hours of purchase.

Clams, mussels, and oysters are usually displayed in their shells on beds of shaved ice, though sometimes you will see them in oxygenated tanks. Their shells should never be gaping or chipped. Freshly shucked meats should be plump, sitting in their own clear liquor on their own half shell. If fresh meats are sold in containers, check for clarity of packing liquid (no cloudiness or foam) and freshness of odor (no ammonia and/or overly "fishy" smell).

Place bivalves (clams, mussels, and oysters) in cool salty water to cover, to help purge them of sand and sediment.

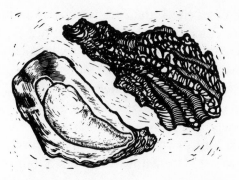

Leave for 30 minutes, and then change the water. When they are purged, drain and use immediately, or store in a bowl or pan in the refrigerator for up to 6 hours.

Scallops are rarely brought to market in their shells. It is usually the muscle meat that is displayed. The larger meats are from sea scallops, the smaller ones from bay scallops. Depending upon the diet of the scallops, their color varies from pearly white to a slight orange cast to pale pink. The meats should be moist, with a translucent sheen; the meats should never be set directly on crushed ice. The odor should be pleasantly briny, never with a trace of ammonia.

Rinse the scallops in cold water and pat dry before using. You can store scallops up to 6 to 8 hours if they are loosely wrapped in parchment or waxed paper and refrigerated.

FROZEN
SHELLFISH

Nearly all the **shrimp** that are sold in markets in America today have been previously frozen. They have had their heads removed, but their tails, shells, and legs should be intact; missing parts means rough handling and probably bruised flesh. A chalky appearance means "freezer burn" and a tough, rubbery texture. The odor should be pleasantly briny, never ammonia-like.

Frozen uncooked shrimp are usually sold already defrosted. Rinse under fresh cold water, pat dry, and use immediately; or store, loosely covered with parchment or waxed paper, in the refrigerator for up to 6 to 8 hours. Shrimp should never be refrozen.

Occasionally **cooked lobster meat and cooked shrimp** have been frozen in transit. Defrost in the refrigerator, blot away any liquid, and use immediately.

Shucked oyster meats and lump crabmeat are often pasteurized and tinned. The packing liquid should be entirely clear, with no foam. These canlike containers must be kept refrigerated at all times. After opening, use immediately, or transfer any leftovers to a clean glass jar and refrigerate in the packing liquid for up to 12 hours.

PACKAGED
FRESH
SHELLFISH

Most people who fish for sport are well aware of local regulations and of the rules of proper storage, but here are two reminders: (1) Ice the fish right away, and keep it packed in plenty of ice until you get home. (2) If you are using a holding tank, change the water often to ensure a steady supply of oxygen and to keep the water temperature cool.

FOR THOSE WHO
CATCH THEIR
OWN FISH

Sea Stocks and Soups

Basic recipes for making stock,
plus a few hearty chowders and soups
and several delicate clear broths

Basic Sea Stock

(*Dashi*)

Makes 1 quart

Most soups and simmered dishes in Japan are based on a sea stock. This classic version calls for only two ingredients—*kombu* (kelp) and *katsuo bushi* (fish flakes). Unlike so many stocks that take hours of slow simmering, this sea stock takes just a few minutes to make. Timing is crucial here: Just as the water comes to a boil, the kelp gives forth its delicate salty-sweet taste, and moments after the fish flakes have been added to the hot kelp broth, they release their smoky flavor into the stock. Strained immediately at its peaks of flavor, the stock is clear and delightful.

Since *dashi* loses its delicate aroma and subtle flavors when frozen, it's best to make it fresh when you need it. Leftover stock will keep well for 4 or 5 days in the refrigerator.

4½ *cups cold water*

20 *square inches* dashi kombu (*kelp for stock making*)

1 *packet (5 grams)* OR ⅓ *cup loosely packed* katsuo bushi (*dried bonito flakes*)

1. Place the kelp in a 2- to 3-quart pot. Add the water, and over high heat, rapidly bring it just to the point of boiling.

2. Remove the pot from the burner, and sprinkle the bonito flakes over the surface of the water. Let the broth stand for 2–3 minutes, until the flakes begin to sink.

3. Remove the kelp with tongs or chopsticks, and strain the broth immediately through a cloth- or paper-lined colander.

Save the kelp after making stock as it can be recycled in several ways: Kelp added to the water used when cooking rice will add a depth of flavor, especially if the rice is being

Kombu is harvested in the chilly waters off the coast of Hokkaido, Japan's northernmost island. The kind of kelp that is best for making stock is a sturdy but slightly sweet-tasting plant called dashi kombu. It is sun-dried before being packaged, and the color ranges from gray to brown to green, often covered with a whitish film. Strips of varying lengths and widths are packaged together. Since the dried kelp is so light, it is more practical to measure it in square inches than to weigh it. Try to avoid breaking the kelp into many pieces; the broken edges become sticky when making stock.

27

seasoned later to make *sushi* (see *shari* recipe, page 49). Softened kelp can also be cooked as a vegetable; it tastes somewhat like fennel or anise (see Fancy Kelp Knots, page 228).

Softened kelp can be kept for a week to 10 days if you do the following: (1) Rinse it under cold water immediately after removing it from the stockpot. (2) Drain the kelp and pat it dry on paper towels. (3) Store the kelp in a closed glass container or plastic bag. (4) Keep it in the vegetable compartment of your refrigerator.

Smoky Sea Stock

(*Tosa Dashi*)

Makes 1 quart

The waters of Tosa Bay, off the Kōchi coast, teem with a tuna-like fish called *katsuo,* or bonito. In the early summer months the catch is served fresh, but year-round bonito is dry-roasted to make fish flakes called *katsuo bushi.* These fish flakes are used to make basic sea stock and to add a smoky flavor to a number of other sauces and stocks as well. This stock, named after the bay where bonito is caught, can be used in lieu of the basic sea stock in any recipe.

1 quart dashi (*basic sea stock, page 27*)

2 tablespoons soy sauce

2 tablespoons mirin (*syrupy rice wine*)

1 packet (5 grams) OR *⅓ loosely packed* katsuo bushi
(*dried bonito flakes*)

If you'll be saving the damp fish flakes to make Ocean Confetti (page 217), make sure you press out as much moisture as possible before storing. Cover and refrigerate for up to 5 days, or use right away.

1. Season the basic sea stock with the soy sauce and syrupy rice wine. Bring the mixture to a boil and simmer for 5 minutes.

2. Remove the pot from the heat, and sprinkle the fish flakes over the surface of the seasoned stock. Let the broth stand for 2–3 minutes, until the flakes begin to sink.

3. Strain the broth immediately through a cloth- or paper-lined colander.

Sea-Tangle in *Miso* Soup, Kansai Style

(Wakamé no Miso Shiru, Kansai Fū)

Serves 4

The Japanese have created an infinite number of variations on the theme of *miso* soup. This marvelous combination of *wakamé* (sea-tangle) and *abura agé* (fried bean curd) is particularly popular throughout the Kansai area, which includes the centrally located cities of Kyoto and Osaka. This Kansai-style soup is a favorite item on many Japanese restaurant menus here in America.

> 3½ *cups* dashi *(basic sea stock, page 27)*
> 1 *teaspoon soy sauce*
> ½ *teaspoon* mirin *(syrupy rice wine)*
> ⅓–½ *packet (5 grams) of dried* wakamé *(sea-tangle)*
> 1 *piece (about 2 × 4½")* abura agé *(fried bean curd)*
> 3–4 *tablespoons* shiro miso *(light fermented bean paste)*
> 1 *slender scallion*

1. Season the stock with the soy sauce and syrupy rice wine and heat it through over medium heat.

2. Soak the dried sea-tangle in cold water for 10 minutes while finishing the soup.

3. Bring a small pot of water to a rolling boil and blanch the fried bean curd in it for 20 seconds to remove surface oil. Drain, and let it cool. Slice the bean curd sheet in half lengthwise, then across into thin strips. When you can handle the bean curd comfortably, gather the strips into a ball in your hand and squeeze out all excess liquid.

4. Add the bean curd strips to the hot seasoned stock. Simmer for 2–3 minutes, then remove the pot from the heat.

5. Measure 3 tablespoons of the bean paste into a deep bowl. Ladle out some of the hot stock and pour it over the bean paste. Whisk the bean paste until it is dissolved, then pour it into the soup pot. Stir and taste; if the flavor is not robust enough, dissolve another tablespoon of bean paste in a little stock and add it to the pot.

6. Trim the scallion, then chop both white and green parts finely. Place these chopped bits of scallion in a small bowl of cold water for a minute, then drain them and squeeze out all excess liquid. Drain the soaking sea-tangle, too.

7. In each of four individual soup bowls, place one fourth of the sea-tangle and scallions. Stir the hot bean-thickened soup, pour it over the sea-tangle and scallions, and serve immediately.

Japanese-Style Clam Chowder

(*Asari no Miso Wan*)

Serves 4

The Japanese adore clam chowder as much as we do, but their version is quite different from either our creamy New England or our spicy Manhattan style. The Japanese serve the clams in their shells, seasoning and thickening the broth with pungent, rich bean paste. A garnish of fresh chives or scallions completes the dish.

> 3 *dozen littleneck* OR *quahog clams*
>
> 20 *square inches* dashi kombu (*kelp for stock making*)
>
> ¼ *cup* saké (*Japanese rice wine*)
>
> ¼ *cup cold water*
>
> 2–3 *tablespoons* aka miso (*dark fermented bean paste*)
>
> 1 *teaspoon* mirin (*syrupy rice wine*), *optional*
>
> 2 *tablespoons chopped fresh chives*

1. Scrub the clams, then soak them in salted water (1 scant tablespoon of salt for 3–4 cups cold water) for 20–30 minutes to help disgorge any sand. Drain, rinse, and drain again.

2. Place the clams in a large wide-mouthed pot with the kelp, rice wine, and water. Cover, and cook over high heat for 4–5 minutes or until the clams are steamed open (discard any that do not open).

3. Divide the clams among four shallow bowls.

In Japan, "double-footed" bivalves called asari *provide a tasty broth without the meat of the clam losing any flavor. Their small shells have pretty striations and add to the attractiveness of this dish. American littlenecks and quahogs make a fine substitute for the Japanese clams.*

4. Strain the broth through a paper- or cloth-lined colander into a clean pot. You should have about 1 to 1½ cups liquid. Whisk in 2 tablespoons of the bean paste. Taste; if the flavor is not robust enough, whisk in the remaining bean paste. If the broth is very salty, add the syrupy rice wine. Briefly reheat the bean-thickened broth, but do not let it boil.

5. Pour the broth over the clams, and garnish each portion with some chopped chives. Serve immediately.

Oysters in Wintry Broth
(*Kaki no Mizoré Wan*)

The Japanese love the changing of the seasons. Here *mizoré,* which means "sleet," describes the grated *daikon* radish in the broth, evoking winter's icy rains. The crunchiness of the *daikon* contrasts marvelously with the smoothness of the oysters. A touch or horseradish enlivens the savory broth.

Serves 4

   1 dozen large oysters, shucked but with their liquor

   1 tablespoon saké (*Japanese rice wine*)

   2 teaspoons soy sauce

16–20 square inches dashi kombu (*kelp for stock making*)

   3 cups cold water

   1 teaspoon usukuchi shōyu (*light soy sauce*)

 8–10 ounces daikon (*Japanese white radish*)

   1 teaspoon cornstarch

   1 teaspoon cold water

   1 teaspoon wasabi (*Japanese horseradish*) *powder*

   1 scant teaspoon cold water

1. Toss the oysters in the rice wine and let them sit for 5 minutes. Pour in the soy sauce and toss again. Let the oysters sit for another 5 minutes.

2. Place the kelp in a saucepan with the cold water and bring it rapidly to a boil over high heat. Remove the kelp and add the oysters with their marinade. Stir to separate the oysters, and simmer for 2 minutes, until they are barely cooked through. Strain the oyster broth through a cloth- or paper-lined colander into a clean saucepan, reserving the oysters. Wipe each of the oysters, if necessary, to remove any froth clinging to them. Season the broth with the light soy sauce.

3. Peel and grate the radish. Place the grated radish in the center of a clean cloth (muslin or an old white linen handkerchief is fine). Bring the corners of the cloth up to enclose the radish, and squeeze gently to drain off the liquid. Keeping the gratings enclosed, carefully rinse the bag under cold water, and squeeze again to rinse the grated radish of impurities.

4. Combine the cornstarch and water in a small cup, and mix to form a smooth paste. Heat the seasoned oyster broth rapidly, and add the cornstarch mixture. Stir as the broth thickens slightly. Add the squeezed radish gratings to the thickened oyster broth. Return the poached oysters to the soup, and simmer long enough to heat them through. Divide the soup among four bowls.

5. In a small bowl, mix the horseradish powder and cold water to make a paste. Divide the paste into four portions and coax each into a tiny mound. Place one mound on top of each portion of poached Oysters in Wintry Broth; the diner stirs the horseradish into the surrounding broth.

Shrimp in Clear Broth with Fresh *Shiitaké*

(*Ebi no Musubi Wan*)

Serves 4

This soup is a fine example of Japanese cooking at its most elegant: a few delicate, symbolic morsels resting in clear broth. Here each pale pink shrimp is "knotted" by pulling its tail through a slit in the body, and the garnish of flat-leafed parsley or *mitsuba* is also "knotted" by twisting several stalks together. These knots symbolize a binding relationship, and the Japanese might serve this soup to celebrate a wedding or a business merger.

> *4 large shrimp, with shells and tails intact*
>
> *1 teaspoon cornstarch*
>
> *2 teaspoons* saké (*Japanese rice wine*)
>
> *4 large fresh* shiitaké (*dark oak*) *mushrooms* OR *other fresh wild mushrooms such as chanterelles*

GARNISH:

> *8 stalks* mitsuba (*trefoil*) OR *flat-leafed parsley*

BROTH:

> *3 cups* dashi (*basic sea stock, page 27*)
>
> *1 teaspoon* saké (*Japanese rice wine*)
>
> *1½ teaspoons* usukuchi shōyu (*light soy sauce*)
>
> *¼ teaspoon salt*

1. Remove the shells from the shrimp, keeping the last segment and the tail intact. With a knife make a shallow slit down the curved back and remove the vein. Turn each shrimp over and make a shallow slit the length of the belly. Gently exert pressure to flatten and "butterfly" each shrimp. With the point of the knife make a deep ¼-inch slit ½ inch from the head end to make a vertical hole. Carefully curl each

shrimp and thread its tail through this hole so that the shrimp is knotted upon itself. Each tail should fan out slightly where it emerges through the hole.

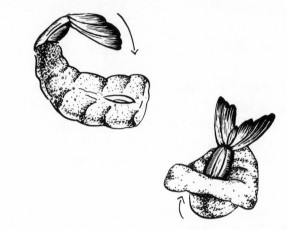

2. Mix the cornstarch with the rice wine, and toss the shrimp in this mixture. Bring a small pot of water to a rolling boil and blanch two of the coated shrimp for 1½ minutes. With a slotted spoon, remove the shrimp and place them on paper towels. Cook the remaining two knotted shrimp. Place a shrimp in each of four bowls.

3. Remove the mushroom stems and reserve them for flavoring the broth. Wipe the caps to remove any traces of grit. Cut each cap in half, slightly on the diagonal, and set the pieces aside.

4. Fill a small bowl with boiling water and dip the stems of the trefoil or parsley in the water to wilt them. Be careful not

to wilt the leaves. When the stems are pliable, take two stalks and lay them parallel to each other, leaves facing the same direction. Loop the stems over your finger and knot them together about ¾ inch below the leaves. Trim the bottom of the stems to make them even. Repeat to make three more knotted garnishes. Set the four green knots aside.

5. Prepare the broth: Heat the stock in a saucepan. Season it with the rice wine, soy sauce, and salt. Add the mushroom stems, and simmer the broth for 5–10 minutes; add the mushroom caps for the final 3–5 minutes. Skim away any froth. Discard the stems.

6. Place two pieces of mushroom cap and a single green knot in each bowl, then gently ladle hot broth over all the ingredients. Serve immediately.

Ocean Pearl in Broth

(Umi no Shinju Wan)

Serves 4

This soup features a gingery quenelle-like seafood dumpling. In Japan it is usually served in a covered bowl; when you remove the lid and see the dumpling, it's as if you have discovered a pearl in an oyster.

SURIMI *(seafood forcemeat)*:

- *6 ounces bay OR sea scallops*
- *4 ounces turbot OR fillet of sole*
- *2 teaspoons cornstarch*
- *2 teaspoons cold water*
- *1 teaspoon ginger juice (extracted from grated fresh ginger)*
- *scant ¼ teaspoon salt*
- *1 small egg white*

POACHING LIQUID:

- *3 cups water*
- *10 square inches* dashi kombu *(kelp for stock making)*
- *1 teaspoon* saké *(Japanese rice wine)*

BROTH:

- *3 cups* dashi *(basic sea stock, page 27)*
- *1 tablespoon* usukuchi shōyu *(light soy sauce)*
- *¼ teaspoon salt*
- *1 teaspoon* saké *(Japanese rice wine)*

THICKENER:

- *1 tablespoon cornstarch*
- *1 tablespoon cold water*

GARNISHES:

1 small bunch fresh kaiwaré *(radish sprouts)* OR *8 tufts blanched broccoli rabe*

1 large, blemish-free lemon (only the peel will be used)

1. Make the seafood forcemeat: Rinse the scallops to make sure no grit clings to them. Pat them dry. Cut the turbot or sole into 1-inch pieces. In a food processor fitted with the metal blade, pulse/process the scallops and fish to make a smooth paste.

2. Combine the cornstarch and water in a small cup, and mix to form a smooth paste. Add the cornstarch mixture to the seafood, and pulse/process to blend. Add the ginger juice, salt, and egg white, and pulse/process until smooth.

3. Make the poaching liquid: Combine the water, kelp, and rice wine in a saucepan. Bring the water rapidly to a boil over high heat. Remove the kelp.

4. With hands wet with water, form the seafood paste into four spheres. Poach them, one at a time, at a moderate boil for 3 minutes in the poaching liquid. The dumplings will puff up a bit and rise to the surface when cooked. You can check by inserting a toothpick in the center of the dumpling: The toothpick should come out clean. Remove the dumplings with a slotted spoon and carefully drain off excess liquid. Place one dumpling in each of four bowls.

5. Rinse out the saucepan, and then add the broth ingredients. Simmer for 2–3 minutes. While the broth is simmering, combine the cornstarch and water to form a smooth paste. Then raise the heat to high, pour in the thickener (the cornstarch mixture), and stir until thickened (about 1 minute).

6. With a zester or small paring knife, remove four long spiral pieces of lemon peel. Wind the peel around the radish sprouts or broccoli rabe tufts as though they were being tied up with a ribbon or streamers.

7. Arrange a bunch of tied greens on top of each "ocean pearl" dumpling. Pour the thickened broth carefully over the arrangement, so it is barely suspended in the broth. Serve immediately.

Broth with Squid and Vegetables

Inochi Wan

Serves 4

I first sampled this invigorating soup in Wajima, at the tip of the Noto Peninsula, which juts out into the Sea of Japan. It was part of my morning meal, served in a lovely ceramic pot set upon a portable burner. The woman serving it told me that this broth is reputed to cure hangover as well as restore sapped energy from arduous travels. After a long hot bath in a deep cedar tub and a night of sound sleep on downy *futon* mattresses, I didn't really need to be "restored," but I enjoyed the soup so much, I want to share it with you.

You may prefer to serve the broth on a chilly evening. It's an especially good way to use trimmed-away portions of squid from other recipes such as Squid and Endive Salad with Ginger Vinaigrette (page 126).

¼ teaspoon salt

legs and side flaps from several squid, about 4 ounces

12 square inches dashi kombu (*kelp for stock making*)

4 cups cold water

1 tablespoon saké (*Japanese rice wine*)

3 tablespoons soy sauce

1 tablespoon mirin (*syrupy rice wine*)

2 small white turnips, about 2 ounces each

1 bunch (about 3½ ounces) enokidaké (*slender creamy white mushrooms*) OR *other fresh wild mushrooms*

2 slender scallions

1. Sprinkle the salt over the squid pieces and rub it in well. Rinse the squid under cold water and pat it dry. (This salting improves the texture and flavor of the squid.)

2. Place the squid in a saucepan with the kelp and cold water. Bring the water quickly to a boil over high heat. Remove the kelp, and lower the heat to maintain a steady simmer. Season the broth with the rice wine, soy sauce, and syrupy rice wine, and cook for 5–6 minutes. Then strain the broth through a cloth- or paper-lined colander into a clean saucepan.

3. Peel the turnips and cut them into ½-inch chunks. Add them to the strained broth and simmer for 2 minutes, until barely tender. Skim away any froth.

4. Rinse the bunch of mushrooms well under running cold water. Shake off excess moisture, and trim away the bottom half of the stems. Toss these mushrooms into the simmering broth and cook for 1 minute. Skim away any froth, and remove the pan from the heat.

5. Trim the scallions and cut them, on the diagonal, into thin slices. Stir them into the broth, and serve immediately.

Thick Rice Soup with Crabmeat

Kani Zōsui

Serves 4

The Japanese enjoy thick rice soups, called *zōsui,* as midday snacks or at the end of a meal comprised of many little dishes. *Zōsui* is homey, soothing stuff and is a fine way to use rice left over from another meal. Adding crab enriches the flavor and dresses up the dish to make it welcome at any dinner table.

BROTH:

   4 *cups* dashi (*basic sea stock, page 27*)

   1 *tablespoon* saké (*Japanese rice wine*)

   scant 1 teaspoon salt

   1 *teaspoon* usukuchi shōyu (*light soy sauce*)

   stems from fresh shiitaké (*dark oak*) *mushrooms, below*

   1 *teaspoon ginger juice (extracted from grated fresh ginger)*

   4 *fresh* shiitaké (*dark oak*) *mushrooms*

   2–3 *ounces crabmeat (canned is fine, fresh is better)*

   2–3 *cups cooked rice (leftovers are perfect)*

   1 *bunch* kaiwaré (*radish sprouts*) OR *8 stalks flat-leafed parsley*

   2 *large eggs, beaten*

1. Prepare the broth: Combine the sea stock, rice wine, salt, light soy sauce, and mushroom stems in a saucepan. Bring to a boil, reduce the heat, and simmer for 5 minutes. Skim the froth away and discard the mushroom stems. Add the ginger juice.

2. Wipe the mushroom caps clean and slice them into thin julienne strips. Add them to the broth and continue to simmer. Skim away any froth.

3. Carefully pick over the crabmeat to remove any cartilage. Add the crabmeat to the broth and continue to simmer. Skim away any froth.

4. Place the cooked rice in a strainer and pour cold water over it, breaking up any lumps and rinsing away excess starch. Drain the rice, add it to the broth, and simmer the soup for 2 minutes.

5. Rinse the radish sprouts or flat-leafed parsley, and trim away any roots. Cut the sprout stalks in half or the parsley stalks into 1-inch lengths, and set aside.

6. Raise the heat slightly, stir the soup clockwise, and pour in the beaten eggs. Remove the saucepan from the heat and stir the soup counterclockwise, to make shreds similar to those in egg drop soup.

7. Divide the soup among four bowls, and scatter the sprouts or parsley over each portion. Serve while piping hot.

Noodles and Shrimp
Tempura in Broth

Tempura Soba

Serves 4

This filling soup is enjoyed as a midday snack by many Japanese. Made to serve two, rather than four, you may find it sufficient for lunch or a light supper.

> *1 package (about 10 ounces) dried soba (buckwheat noodles)*

BROTH:

> *3 cups dashi (basic sea stock, page 27)*
>
> *3 tablespoons soy sauce*
>
> *2 tablespoons mirin (syrupy rice wine)*
>
> *1 packet (5 grams) katsuo bushi (dried bonito flakes)*

> *4 batter-fried shrimp (tempura, page 159)*
>
> *1 scallion, trimmed and finely chopped*
>
> *¼ teaspoon schichimi tōgarashi (seven-spice powder)*

1. Over high heat, bring a large pot of water to a rolling boil. Scatter the buckwheat noodles across the water, cover, and return to a boil as rapidly as possible. Add the cold water, cover, and return to a boil again. Cook the noodles for 5 minutes, then test a strand: Place it in cold water to cool, then bite it. The noodle should be cooked through but still firm. If necessary, cook the noodles an additional minute or two, then drain immediately. Rinse the noodles under running cold water to remove surface starch. Set them aside to drain.

2. Prepare the broth: Combine the sea stock, soy sauce, and syrupy rice wine in a saucepan, bring to a boil, and simmer for 2–3 minutes. Remove the pan from the heat and sprinkle in the bonito flakes. Allow the flakes to steep for 3 minutes, or

until they begin to sink. Strain the broth through a paper- or cloth-lined colander.

3. Assembling the dish: Using a microwave oven is the simplest. In each of four microwave-safe deep bowls place one fourth of the noodles, then pour one fourth of the broth over each portion. Cover the bowls with clear plastic wrap, perforate the wrap with a few holes to allow steam to escape, and heat on medium (about 80 percent power or 490 watts) for 1½ minutes.

Remove the bowls from the microwave and set them aside, still lidded with plastic wrap, and line the bottom of the microwave with a double layer of paper towels. Lay the batter-fried shrimp on the paper towels, and then place a single sheet of paper towel over the shrimp. Heat the shrimp on the high setting (full power or 600 watts) for 30–40 seconds. Remove the plastic wrap from the bowls of noodles and place a batter-fried shrimp on top of each.

4. Sprinkle each portion of soup with some chopped scallions and a pinch of seven-spice powder. Serve immediately.

If you do not have a microwave: Heat the broth in a saucepan, then add the noodles and heat through for 1 minute. Divide the broth and noodles among four bowls. Heat the shrimp for 3–4 minutes on a foil-lined rack in a conventional oven preheated to 350 degrees. Place a shrimp on top of each portion of soup, then garnish with scallions and a pinch of seven-spice powder.

After making the broth, save the bonito flakes to use in Ocean Confetti (page 217).

Sushi and Sashimi

The basic recipe for vinegared rice, used in all *sushi* dishes, plus many rolled, tossed, and fancifully molded vinegared-rice recipes and recipes for fresh fish simply sliced and festively garnished

Seasoned Rice for *Sushi*

Shari

Makes 3 cups

Here is the basic recipe for making the vinegared rice essential to all *sushi* recipes. There are three keys to achieving the best taste and texture: **(1) Use short-grained rice,** preferably the Japanese-style rice grown in California (Kokuho Rose, Blue Rose, and Kotobuki are among the most readily available brands). **(2) Use freshly cooked rice,** still warm and therefore more receptive to absorbing the seasoned vinegar. **(3) Do not refrigerate the seasoned rice.** *Sushi* rice is a naturally preserved food (in fact, that is how it became popular in Japan, centuries before refrigeration was possible) and will keep well for many hours in a cool room if covered with a clean damp cloth and/or clear plastic wrap. If refrigerated, it will turn hard and crusty and any attempt to warm it up will result in mushy, tasteless rice.

1½ cups raw Japanese-style short-grained rice

1¾ cups cold water

   softened kelp left over from stock making, optional

¼–⅓ cup sushi su *(seasoned rice vinegar)*

1. Place the rice in a bowl and cover it with cold water. Stir vigorously to wash the rice clear of excess starch. Strain the rice and repeat the washing procedure with fresh cold water until the rinsing water runs clear. This usually takes two or three rinsings. Drain the rice well after the final rinsing.

2. Place the rice in a sturdy, straight-sided 3- to 4-quart pot. (If you have a piece of kelp left over from making stock, lay it over the rice for added flavor.) Measure in the 1¾ cups fresh cold water. Ideally, let the rice sit in its cooking water for 10 minutes before cooking it. If pressed for time, add ½ teaspoon more water. Cover the pot with a tight-fitting lid.

3. Over high heat, bring the water in the pot to a rolling boil. It's best not to remove the lid to check on its progress. Instead, rely on other clues: You can hear the bubbling noises and see the lid begin to dance. This should take about 5 minutes. Reduce the heat and continue to cook at a simmer until the water is absorbed (about 5 minutes longer); you may hear a low hissing sound. Increase the heat to high again for 30 seconds, to dry off the rice. Remove the pot, still tightly covered, from the heat and let the rice stand for at least 10 minutes, or up to 30 minutes. This final self-steaming makes more tender grains of rice.

4. Transfer the cooked rice to a large bowl. (The Japanese use a wide wooden tub called a *handai* or *sushi oké,* which is ideal. But a wide-mouthed glass or ceramic bowl is fine, especially if it has a wide flat bottom. Avoid metal since it tends to retain heat.) Toss the rice while fanning it, to cool it without condensation forming. (The Japanese use a flat lacquered fan called an *uchiwa,* but a piece of cardboard is just as useful.) Use a wooden spoon to toss the rice (the Japanese use a paddle-like one called a *shamoji*).

5. When there are no more clouds of steam rising from the rice, begin to toss it with the seasoned vinegar, starting with just a tablespoonful. Using gentle folding and tossing motions, gradually season the rice with more of the vinegar. Taste a bit of rice after using ¼ cup of the seasoned vinegar; if it still tastes bland, add the remaining vinegar. Cover the seasoned rice with a damp cloth until you are ready to use it.

raw rice	cooking water	seasoned vinegar	yield
1 cup	1 cup plus 2 tablespoons	scant ¼ cup =	**2 cups**
2 cups	2⅓ cups	scant ½ cup =	**4 cups**
2½ cups	scant 2¾ cups	generous ½ cup =	**5 cups**

To make more, or less, shari seasoned rice, use the accompanying chart to alter quantities. The procedure remains the same.

If you cannot find already seasoned vinegar, you can make it yourself. Combine the ingredients in a small saucepan and heat, stirring, just until the sugar and salt dissolve. Refrigerate any leftovers in a lidded glass or ceramic jar.

   1 cup rice vinegar (OR ¾ cup distilled white vinegar, 2 tablespoons water, and 1 tablespoon fresh lemon juice)

   1½ tablespoons sugar

   1 teaspoon salt

Tuna, Shrimp, and Salmon Petal *Sushi*

Hanabira-Zushi

Makes 42 bite-size pieces

This is a wonderful dish for entertaining—even guests who are new to the pleasures of Japanese food love these bite-size tuna, cooked shrimp, and smoked salmon *sushi*. And since the dish can be made several hours ahead of your guests' arrival, it gives you plenty of time to lavish on the presentation. The Japanese often use seasonal motifs in arranging their food, and here the red, pink, and orange-toned *sushi* resemble spring blossom petals.

> 3½–4 *cups* shari (*seasoned rice for* sushi)
>
> 6 *large shrimp, with shells and tails intact*
>
> 1 *teaspoon* saké (*Japanese rice wine*)
>
> 4–6 *ounces fresh* sashimi-*quality* maguro (*tuna*), *purchased in a block from a Japanese food store*
>
> 2–3 *ounces smoked salmon, in broad thin slices*
>
> 1–2 *teaspoons* wasabi (*Japanese horseradish*) *powder*
>
> *soy sauce for dipping, optional*

1. Divide the seasoned rice into 42 small portions, and with moistened hands and/or a damp cloth, coax the rice into small balls. Cover these with a damp cloth while preparing the toppings.

2. Remove the vein from each shrimp as best you can by tugging gently on it from the head end. Insert a short bamboo skewer or a round toothpick through the back of each shrimp, just under the shell, to straighten it out.

3. Bring a small pot of water to a rolling boil, and add the rice wine. Blanch the skewered shrimp for 2–2½ minutes after the water returns to a boil. Remove the shrimp immediately,

and while they are still warm, peel them *before* removing the skewers. To remove the skewers or toothpicks, twirl them in place to loosen, then pull them out. Slit each shrimp along the belly (white, unstriped side) to "butterfly" it, and press to flatten it into a triangular shape. Cut each shrimp in half; the top piece will be a small triangle. Set aside the twelve pieces. This can be done the day before; refrigerate until ready to use.

4. Slice the tuna into thin (about 1/16-inch) slices. If the slices are longer than 1½ inches, cut them in half. Ideally you should have eighteen thin pieces, each about 1¼ inches square. Set aside.

5. Cut the smoked salmon into twelve pieces, each about 1¼ inches square. Set aside.

6. Mix the horseradish powder with an equal amount of cold water, and stir to make a paste.

7. Each ball of rice will be draped with a topping (shrimp, tuna, or smoked salmon) and rounded to look like a spring blossom petal: Cut out 42 pieces of clear plastic wrap, each about 2½ inches square. Lay a piece of shrimp (white side up, striped side down), salmon, or tuna in the center of each square. Place a dab of *wasabi* paste on each piece of shrimp, salmon, or tuna. Then place a ball of seasoned rice on each. Lifting up the edges of the plastic wrap, enclose the fish and rice, twisting the edges to make a snug, perfect ball shape. Keep the balls tied snugly in plastic wrap for at least 15

minutes, and up to 1½ hours, in a cool spot in the kitchen. (Don't refrigerate or place directly on ice. If you are concerned about the temperature, fill a roasting pan with ice and a bit of water. Set your platter or tray of wrapped *sushi* over the roasting pan.)

8. Just before serving, remove the plastic wrap and arrange the *sushi*, fish up, on a serving platter. You can cluster the *sushi* balls by type—all the tuna in one spot, the shrimp in another, and the salmon separate too—or arrange a mixture. Provide soy sauce for dipping, if you like.

Two-Toned Caviar *Sushi*

Ni Shoku-Zushi

Sushi bars throughout Japan and America serve a wide variety of *nigiri-zushi*, which are compact ovals of rice on which a fresh slice of fish, such as tuna or fluke, is draped. Fish roes, which are also marvelous eaten with *sushi* rice, need a collar of paper-thin seaweed to keep them balanced atop the rice. This recipe makes colorful pairs of fish roe *sushi*—large red globes of salmon caviar and smaller crystal-line globes of golden whitefish caviar. Both varieties are garnished with a bit of bright green cucumber to make the final presentation even more dramatic.

Makes 30 bite-size pieces

4 cups shari (*seasoned rice for* sushi, *page 49*)

5 full sheets yaki nori (*paper-thin toasted seaweed*)

1 small (about 3–4 ounces) slender Kirby OR *other unwaxed cucumber*

pinch salt

1 tablespoon wasabi (*Japanese horseradish*) *powder*

scant 1 tablespoon cold water

4 ounces ikura (*red salmon caviar*)

4 ounces golden whitefish caviar

soy sauce for dipping, optional

1. Divide the rice into thirty portions. With damp hands, mold each portion into a compact oval-shaped nugget, or use the mold described on page 57.

2. Cut each sheet of *nori* into six strips, each 7½ by 1½ inches; 30 strips in all. Stack these in a dry location.

3. Make thirty cucumber "fans": Wash the cucumber well without bruising it, since the green skin will be eaten. Slice off

the stem (darker) end of the cucumber, and rub this piece in a circular motion over the cut end of the cucumber, to remove what the Japanese call *aku*, or bitterness, which appears as a white foam. Rinse the foam away and trim off the other end of the cucumber.

Slice the cucumber in half lengthwise, and scrape out the seeds. Place each cucumber half, flat side down, on a chopping board. Lay a disposable wooden chopstick on each side of one cucumber half to keep the knife from slicing all the way through. With a very sharp knife, make as many extremely fine slits in the cucumber as possible. Repeat the procedure with the other half. Sprinkle salt over the slit sides, then gently rub it in to wilt the cucumber halves. A wavy pattern should appear.

Rinse the cucumber halves in cold water and pat them dry. Slice each half lengthwise, to yield four slits sticks. When you

press on the slits, the cucumber will fan out. Cut out thirty pieces, each with five to eight segments to its fan. Each of these will be used in a single *sushi* oval.

4. Mix the horseradish powder with the cold water to make a paste. Dab a bit of this paste on top of each rice oval.

5. To form each piece of *sushi*, take an oval of rice and wind a single strip of seaweed around it to make a collar, much like a soufflé collar. Seal the end of the *nori* with a grain or two of rice.

6. Lay a cucumber fan in the corner of each oval. Fill the remaining space with caviar; fifteen pieces should be filled with red salmon roe, and fifteen pieces with the golden whitefish caviar.

7. Serve on a large hors d'oeuvres tray, or as pairs on a small plate as a first course to a large meal. Serve soy sauce on the side, if you wish, for dipping.

Many modern Japanese homemakers use a plastic mold to help shape the rice into compact ovals. Called sushi-gata, *these molds are sold in many Oriental grocery stores in America, and they simplify the task tremendously. The mold comes in two pieces: The bottom has five wells or compartments, each with an oval hole in it. The lid is segmented into five compartments and has a bar across the top. Separate the bottom from the lid and dip both in a bowl of cold water. Place the bottom half, holes down, on a clean cutting board. Fill the compartments with rice to just above the segmenting barriers. Cover with the lid, pressing down firmly on the crossbar. Remove the lid, invert the rice-stuffed bottom, and tap out the rice ovals. If any stick stubbornly, gently poke through the holes in the compartments. Repeat five times to make thirty ovals in all.*

Peppery Smoked Eel *Sushi*

Anago-Zushi

Makes 1 dozen pieces

If you've never tried smoked eel before, you'll be surprised at how rich and meaty this rather delicately textured fish can be. Several varieties of precooked smoked eel are available in Oriental food stores, usually stored in the freezer case. For this particular dish *anago* is the best choice, though *unagi* is fine too. Some brands of eel come packed with their own *taré*, or sauce, but since not all do, I've included a recipe for making a simple soy glaze.

4 *ounces* anago *or* unagi (*cooked smoked eel*)

TARÉ (SAUCE):

    2 *tablespoons soy sauce*

    3 *tablespoons* mirin (*syrupy rice wine*)

    1 *teaspoon* wasabi (*Japanese horseradish*) *powder*

    1 *teaspoon cold water*

1¼ *cups* shari (*seasoned rice for* sushi, *page 49*)

    1 *tablespoon* sanshō no mi (*pepper berries*), *crushed* OR *scant* ½ *teaspoon* sanshō (*fragrant Japanese pepper*)

    1 *tablespoon* amazu shōga (*pink pickled ginger*) OR beni shōga (*red pickled ginger*)

1. Defrost the smoked eel in your refrigerator. Brush the flesh side with some of the glazing sauce, then place it under a broiler for 2 minutes. Paint additional glazing sauce over the eel, broil another minute, and paint again. Let the eel come to room temperature.

2. If your package of eel did not have additional sauce, make some by combining the soy sauce and syrupy rice wine in a

small saucepan. Simmer over medium heat 6–7 minutes until foamy and slightly thickened. Skim off the pale froth. Allow the glaze-like sauce to cool in the pan (any leftovers will keep well for several days if covered and refrigerated).

3. Line a glass or metal loaf, pâté, or terrine pan with clear plastic wrap. (The Japanese have a special box-shaped mold for shaping this kind of *sushi;* it is described here for those who wish to use one.) Make sure the wrap extends well beyond the sides of the mold or pan. Arrange the eel, flesh down and skin side up, on the bottom of the mold or pan. Trim and patch the strip of eel, if necessary, to cover the bottom entirely.

The Japanese use an oshi-gata mold for shaping loaf sushi dishes. Made from wood, they can be found for sale at Oriental groceries throughout the United States. They come in a variety of sizes and shapes; the narrow rectangular ones are best for this type of sushi. Soak the mold in cold water for a few minutes before using it, and wash it with a mild detergent after use. Rinse and let it dry naturally. Store the wooden mold in a closed plastic bag or container if you live in a dry climate.

4. Mix the horseradish powder with the cold water to make a paste. Spread this paste evenly over the eel skin.

5. Fill the mold or pan with the seasoned rice, pressing with moistened fingers to compact the rice and make it even. Fold the clear plastic wrap over the rice.

6. Cut a piece of heavy cardboard to fit inside your pan (this is in lieu of the lid piece of a Japanese mold). Place heavy objects, such as cans, jars, or potatoes, on the lid to weight it down. Five to 8 pounds of pressure, evenly distributed, is ideal.

7. Allow the *sushi* to sit for at least 1 hour, or up to 5 or 6 hours, in a cool spot in your kitchen. When you are ready to unmold it, remove the weights and invert the mold. For cleaner, sharper edges, slice the *sushi* into smaller pieces while it is still wrapped. Slice the loaf lengthwise, then across five times, to yield one dozen pieces in all. Wipe your knife on a damp cloth between slices. Unwrap the *sushi* and paint the top of each piece with a bit of sauce. Then garnish each piece with a few crushed pepper berries or a generous sprinkling of fragrant pepper.

8. Serve with pink or red pickled ginger on the side. No additional soy sauce is needed.

Mini Plump Rolls
Mini Futo Maki-Zushi

Makes 6 rolls,
yielding 24 pieces

A festive dish in their native land, these colorful *sushi* rolls easily share the limelight with a wide variety of hors d'oeuvres, Japanese and otherwise. They are particularly good with the Japanese Seafood Terrine (page 106) or the Mussels with Mustard Sauce and Scallions (page 112). Or try pairing Mini Plump Rolls with any of the other *sushi* dishes in this section, such as Tuna, Shrimp, and Salmon Petal *Sushi* (page 52) or Peppery Smoked Eel *Sushi* (page 58). Plump Rolls make terrific picnic fare, too, since they can be made hours before eating.

The rolling instructions given here make use of half-sheets

of *nori* seaweed since they are easier to handle when you are first developing your rolling skills. The fillings are typical of the ingredients that the Japanese like to combine into such "plump rolls."

3 *cups* shari (*seasoned rice for* sushi, *page 49*)

3 *full sheets* yaki nori (*paper-thin toasted seaweed*)

1 *large Paper-Thin Omelet* (*page 67*)

48 *inches Sweet Simmered Gourd Ribbons* (*page 65*)

½ *cup Rosy Flaked Fish* (*page 64*)

18 *stalks flat-leafed parsley*

¼ *teaspoon salt*

½ *tablespoon white sesame seeds*

GARNISH:

amazu shōga (*pink pickled ginger*), *drained*

soy sauce for dipping, optional

1. With damp hands, divide the seasoned rice into six portions, and shape each into a roughly oblong mass about 3 inches long. Set these aside, covered with a damp cloth.

2. Cut the sheets of *nori* in half, to yield six half-sheets; stack these in a dry location. Cut the omelet into six wedges, then cut each wedge into ½-inch-wide strips. Cut the gourd ribbon into twelve, 4-inch lengths. Divide the rosy flaked fish into six portions.

3. Rinse the parsley carefully under cold water. Divide it into three bunches, keeping all the sprigs running in the same direction. Tie the bunches with string around the stems. Bring several cups of water to a rolling boil, add the salt (to heighten the color), and quickly dip the bunches of parsley into it. Drain immediately, running cold water over the parsley to stop the cooking process. Squeeze out all excess water and pat

the parsley dry. Trim the parsley, discarding the string and root ends. Divide each bunch in half, to make six portions.

4. Place the sesame seeds in a dry skillet over fairly high heat. Shaking the skillet slightly, toast the seeds until a few pop or they just begin to color, about 30–40 seconds.

5. Lay one sheet of seaweed, rough side up and with one of the shorter sides facing you, on a slatted bamboo mat. With damp hands, spread one portion of rice across the lower two thirds of the seaweed. Make a colorful striped pattern across the rice with your fillings: egg shreds (several ribbons for each roll), simmered gourd ribbons (two per roll), rosy flaked fish (one portion per roll), and blanched flat-leafed parsley (three stalks per roll).

6. Lifting the mat, begin to roll the *sushi* away from you. Flip it up and over, snugly enclosing the fillings. Continue to roll, lifting the mat and pushing the *sushi* away from you at the same time. When you get to the far end, press a few grains of rice to the edge of the seaweed before completing the roll, to seal the edge.

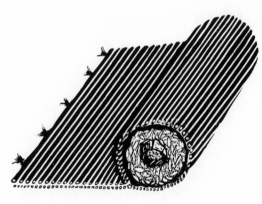

7. With a sharp knife, slice each roll in half crosswise, and then cut each half into two slices. Wipe your knife blade on a damp cloth between cuts. Serve the rolls at room temperature with a garnish of pink pickled ginger, and soy sauce for dipping if you like.

Rosy Flaked Fish
Sakura Dembu

Makes 1 generous cup, enough for 8 mini rolls of sushi

The name *sakura dembu* literally means "cherry blossom flaked fish," and it is a popular addition to rolled *sushi*, particularly in the springtime when picnic menus echo nature's glory. Commercially prepared *sakura dembu* tends to be too sweet for American tastes, and sometimes the color is more than just blushing. Although it takes a bit of time to make *sakura dembu*, it's not very difficult. And since it will keep for a month or more if well refrigerated, I urge you to try making your own rosy flaked fish to use in colorful *sushi* rolls.

4–6 *ounces scrod* OR *other mild-flavored white-flesh fish*

2 *teaspoons* saké (*Japanese rice wine*)

1 *tiny drop red food coloring*

1 *tablespoon* mirin (*syrupy rice wine*)

scant ¼ teaspoon salt

1. Cut the fish into 1- to 2-inch pieces. Sprinkle 1 teaspoon of the rice wine over the fish, and add the other teaspoonful to a small pot of boiling water. Blanch the fish for 2 minutes in the vigorously boiling liquid, skimming off any froth from the surface. Drain the fish and let it cool naturally until you can handle it comfortably. Remove all skin, bones, and/or cartilage from the fish.

2. Place the cooked fish in the bowl of a food processor fitted with a metal blade. Pulse/process to flake the fish. Combine the food coloring and the syrupy rice wine in a small cup and stir well. Add this to the fish, and pulse/process to combine it well. Add the salt and pulse/process to distribute it well, too.

3. Place the seasoned and tinted fish mixture in a dry non-stick skillet over low heat and slowly roast it until dry

and fluffy, stirring frequently to break up lumps and prevent scorching. This dry-roasting may take up to 15 or 20 minutes. Patience is necessary, and increased heat cannot help speed the process.

4. Turn the rosy-colored fish flakes out on a clean dry plate, and allow to cool to room temperature. If you are not using it all at once, store the *sakura dembu* in an airtight container in the refrigerator for future use. It will keep for at least 1 month.

Sweet Simmered Gourd Ribbons

Kampyō no Umani

The Japanese often use dried gourd strips to tie up packets of food. The simmered strips are also a popular filling for rolled *sushi*. Since the cooked gourd ribbon keeps well (for a week to 10 days, refrigerated), I suggest you make an entire package and save any leftovers for future use.

Makes several yards

   1 packet (about 1 ounce) kampyō *(gourd strips)*
   ½ teaspoon salt
   ½ cup dashi *(basic sea stock, page 27)*
   3 tablespoons sugar
   3 tablespoons soy sauce

1. Soak the gourd strips in warm water to cover for 10 minutes. Drain, and rub with the salt to soften the fibrous strips. Rinse off the salt, and blanch the strips in boiling water to cover for 8–10 minutes. Drain, but do *not* refesh under cold water.

2. In a small saucepan, combine the sea stock, sugar, and soy sauce. Bring it to a boil over medium heat, stirring to dissolve the sugar. Add the gourd strips and cook, adjusting the heat if necessary to maintain a steady but gentle bubbling. Cook the gourd, preferably using an *otoshi-buta* (see explanation at left), for 8–10 minutes or until the simmering liquid is nearly gone. Stir and turn over the gourd strips occasionally to ensure even coloration while cooking (especially important if you do not have a dropped lid). Allow the gourd strips to cool in the cooking pot. Before using, drain the strips of excess liquid. Cover and refrigerate if not using immediately.

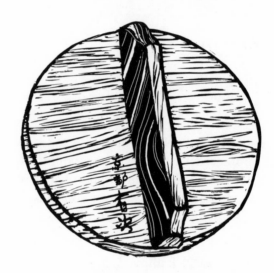

Paper-Thin Omelet

Usutamago Yaki

This basic recipe makes crepe-like sheets which the Japanese use in a variety of ways: several recipes in this book call for them. Learning how to flip the omelet with a single chopstick may take a few tries, but once you've mastered the technique, you'll find it a marvelous and useful skill.

Makes 4–5 large (8-inch) circles or 6–8 small (6-inch) circles

3–4 *extra-large eggs*

  1 *tablespoon* saké (*Japanese rice wine*)

  1 *teaspoon sugar*

⅛ *teaspoon salt*

  1 *teaspoon cornstarch mixed with 1 tablespoon cold water, optional*

  vegetable oil for seasoning pan, optional

1. Break the eggs into a bowl and season them with the rice wine, sugar, and salt. Beat to mix thoroughly, but try not to incorporate air as you do this. Pour the egg mixture through a mesh strainer to ensure a smooth yellow mixture.

2. If you want to strengthen the paper-thin omelet (for use in Golden Purse *Sushi*, page 72, for example), add the cornstarch paste. Stir the paste into the egg mixture to combine it well.

3. For this omelet I recommend using a skillet with a non-stick surface such as Teflon or SilverStone. Even so, I season it with a thin layer of oil, re-oiling the pan between sheets by wiping it with a small wad of paper towel dipped in vegetable oil. An 8-inch skillet is best for making the larger circles for use in Golden Purse *sushi*; small circles from a 6-inch pan are fine when the omelet will be shredded later for any of the other *sushi* dishes. Heat your skillet over medium heat.

4. Pour a little less than one quarter of the egg mixture into the skillet to make the larger circles; about half that for the smaller ones. Add the measured egg mixture to the pan all at once. Swirl this mixture to cover the surface of the skillet evenly. Keep it over medium heat until the edges seem to dry a bit. Remove the skillet from the heat and let the egg sheet cook by retained heat for another 20–30 seconds before flipping it over.

5. The Japanese use a single chopstick to help flip their sheets of omelet. Trace completely around the circumference of the omelet with the tip of your chopstick. Then, holding the skillet in one hand and the chopstick in the other, tilt the pan so that your hands face each other. Insert the tip of your chopstick just under the edge of the omelet, and alternate the use of twirling motions with back-and-forth strokes to work your way across to the other side of the pan. Lift the omelet, draped over the chopstick, and lay it back in the pan, inverted. Allow the other side to dry off (at most 30 seconds additional exposure to heat), then flip it out of the skillet. Continue to make the omelets in the same manner, stacking them as you go. Thin omelets such as these will keep for 5 days, covered and refrigerated.

Tricolored Streamer *Sushi*

Tazuna-Zushi

A literal translation of the Japanese word *tazuna* ("horse rein") might make you think this *sushi* dish had some equestrian connection. Actually, the name is meant to conjure up a twisted streamer-like strip of leather. The diagonal striped pattern created by the smoked salmon, omelet, and flat-leafed parsley is such that these bite-size pieces of *sushi* have a rather festive look.

This is a challenging preparation, and until you've rolled a few, it may be difficult to shape well. It's worth the effort of practicing, though, since the end result is so impressive and the ingredients themselves are not very costly.

> 2 ounces smoked salmon, in thin, broad, brightly colored slices
>
> 1 large Paper-Thin Omelet (*page 67*)
>
> 10–12 stalks flat-leafed parsley
>
> 1 teaspoon drained and finely minced amazu shōga (*pink pickled ginger*)
>
> 1 cup shari (*seasoned rice for* sushi, *page 49*)

1. Cut the salmon into ½-inch-wide strips, each about 3–4 inches long. Then cut the omelet into ¾-inch-wide strips, each about 3 or 4 inches long.

2. Tie the stalks of parsley together and dip the leaves into boiling salted water to quickly blanch and wilt them. Refresh under cold water and pat dry with paper towels. Trim away the stems.

3. You will need three pieces of clear plastic wrap, each measuring 6 by 8 inches. Arrange the first piece of wrap on a *sudaré* (bamboo mat for rolling *sushi*) so that it runs 8 inches across and 6 inches high.

4. Arrange the ingredients to form diagonal stripes across the center of the plastic wrap. Alternate parsley, omelet, and salmon, overlapping the ingredients slightly and spreading the leaves of the parsley when you lay them down. Repeat the pattern of green (parsley), yellow (omelet), and orange-pink (salmon) again. The entire tricolored band should be about 6 inches across.

5. Toss the pink pickled ginger into the *sushi* rice. Divide the rice into three portions, and coax each into an oblong 6 inches long. Place a single portion of *sushi* rice over the striped ingredients. Press firmly with your fingertips, making sure that all ingredients are covered with a thin layer of rice.

6. Roll the *sushi* up and away from you, making sure to enclose the roll snugly in clear wrap. Twist the ends to even them off. Repeat the same procedure with the remaining ingredients, to make three rolls in all.

7. With a very sharp knife, cut each roll in half through the plastic wrap. Cut each piece in half again, wiping your knife with a damp towel between cuts. Remove and discard the plastic wrap. Each piece should have at least a bit of each of the three ingredients on top of it.

A sudaré or slatted bamboo mat, is a useful piece of equipment to have in any kitchen. The Japanese use it primarily to help roll sushi dishes such as this one and the Mini Plump Rolls on page 60, but it is terrific for non-Oriental jelly rolls, too. Slatted bamboo mats are available at most Oriental groceries throughout the United States. After each use, wash in warm water with a mild detergent, making sure that no grains of rice are hidden between the slats. Rinse and let dry naturally.

Golden Purse *Sushi*

Chakin-Zushi

Makes 4 pieces

These crepe-wrapped *sushi*, named "golden purse" because they resemble the money pouches that were popular during the feudal era, make a spectacular first course. Since they contain smoked, not fresh, fish they can be made several hours ahead of serving time.

½ *tablespoon white sesame seeds*

¼ *cup flaked smoked fish, skin and bones carefully removed (trout, chubb, or whitefish is best)*

1 *tablespoon drained and finely minced* amazu shōga *(pink pickled ginger)*

2 *cups* shari *(seasoned rice for* sushi, *page 49)*

4 *large Paper-Thin Omelets (page 67)*

35–40 *inches Sweet Simmered Gourd Ribbons (page 65)*

1. Place the sesame seeds in a clean, dry skillet and roast them over medium-high heat for 30–40 seconds, until they pop or color ever so slightly.

2. In a large bowl, toss the flaked fish, ginger, and sesame seeds into the seasoned rice. Divide the rice mixture into four portions. With a damp cloth, mold each portion into a sphere. Cover with a damp cloth.

3. Lay a single omelet on a dry cutting board. Place a single rice sphere in the center. Lift the omelet up around the rice to enclose it, carefully pleating the folds as you go.

4. Secure the pleats by tying the bundle with a gourd ribbon. Repeat to make three more. If you wish to hold the *sushi* for several hours, cover with clear plastic wrap and keep in a cool spot at room temperature.

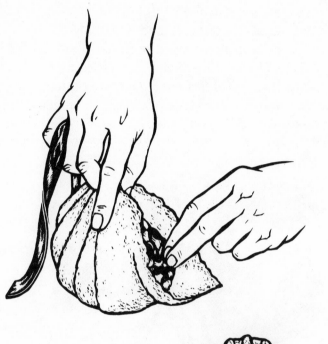

Scattered *Sushi* with Lobster
Robusutā no Chirashi-Zushi

Serves 4–6

Scattered *Sushi* is a dish found more often in homes than in restaurants in Japan, particularly this kind of pilaff-like tossed arrangement. Cooked, pickled, and fresh ingredients are mixed with tartly seasoned cooked rice, then garnished with colorful shreds of paper-thin omelet, vegetables, and seafood. In Japan, large platters of Scattered *Sushi* are brought out to celebrate or commemorate a special event or holiday. This lobster version would be perfect in the summer, perhaps on the Fourth of July.

GARNISHES:

> *3–4 ounces fresh snow peas*
>
> *6 small OR 3 large Paper-Thin Omelets (page 67)*
>
> *2–3 tablespoons drained and shredded* beni shōga *(red pickled ginger)*
>
> *cooked tail meat of 1½-pound lobster, cut into ¼-inch-thick medallions*
>
> *1½ tablespoons white sesame seeds*
>
> *3–5 cups* shari *(seasoned rice for* sushi, *page 49)*

½–⅓ *cup chopped cooked lobster meat* (*claw and legs*)

1½–2 *tablespoons drained and finely minced* amazu shōga (*pink pickled ginger*)

1 *teaspoon* ao nori (*sea herb flakes*), *optional*

1. Snap back the stem of each snow pea to remove the string. In a small saucepan bring several cups of lightly salted water to a rolling boil. Blanch the snow peas for 5 seconds, then drain them and refresh them under cold water. Drain again, and pat the snow peas dry. This can be done an hour or so before serving time. Just before serving, slice the snow peas slightly on the diagonal into thin julienne strips.

2. The paper-thin omelet can be made and refrigerated many days in advance of serving. Just before serving, cut them into narrow julienne shreds.

3. The red pickled ginger should be well drained of its bottled liquid and set on paper towels to avoid staining plates or cutting boards.

4. In a clean dry skillet, roast the sesame seeds over medium-high heat for about 45 seconds, or until they pop or color ever so slightly.

5. In a large bowl, toss the seasoned rice with the toasted sesame seeds, chopped lobster meat, and pink pickled ginger. Sprinkle the sea herb flakes over the rice, too, if you want a more pronounced seashore aroma. Toss gently but thoroughly after each addition to make sure all is well distributed.

6. Lightly mound the rice mixture on a large plate or tray (12 to 20 inches in diameter). Do not let it mound higher than 1½ inches. The dish can be assembled to this point 3–4 hours in advance of serving, as long as you cover it snugly with clear plastic wrap and keep it at room temperature, away from extremes of hot or cold.

7. Have all the *sushi* garnishes ready and waiting on separate plates; the yellow omelet shreds, the red-and-white lobster medallions, the green snow peas, and the shredded red pickled ginger. Just before you serve the dish, garnish the *sushi*: Scatter the egg shreds over the rice to cover the mound completely. Scatter, at random, the lobster meat medallions, then the snow peas, so that the yellow of the egg shows through. Mound the red ginger at the center of the plate. Serve at room temperature.

Fresh Fluke Swirls

Hiramé no Uzumaki

Makes 1 dozen pieces

Translucent slices of fresh fluke and slivers of bright red pickled ginger are wound in a thin spiral of cucumber, then banded with a narrow strip of black seaweed. The resulting bite-size hors d'oeuvres are colorful and scrumptious.

2 straight cucumbers, each about 6 inches long

¼ teaspoon salt

3–4 ounces fresh sashimi-quality fluke or sea bream

1 tablespoon drained and shredded beni shōga (red pickled ginger)

½ sheet yaki nori (paper-thin toasted seaweed)

2 teaspoons wasabi (Japanese horseradish) powder

1½ teaspoons cold water

soy sauce, for dipping

1. Cut off the stem (darker) end of each cucumber and rub the cut surfaces in a circular motion with the sliced-off end pieces. A foamy, pasty white substance will appear. This is what the Japanese refer to as *aku*, or bitterness. Rinse it away.

2. Peel the cucumber with a vegetable peeler, if you like, or use the technique described here to remove the outer skin. Slice the cucumber *katsura muki* style (see explanation here): Cut the cucumber into 1- to 1½-inch lengths. Using slight up-and-down motions, guide a sharp knife through a cucumber piece to create a long (5 inches or longer), wide, continuous strip. Discard (or nibble) the core of seeds at the center. Repeat to make at least six unbroken strips.

3. Lightly salt the cucumber strips and let them sit a few minutes to wilt slightly (this will make them easier to work with later).

4. Remove the skin from the fish if it is still attached: Lay the fish on a clean, dry board, skin side down. Start from the narrow (tail) end and work toward the wider (head) end. Insert the tip of a sharp knife between the skin and the flesh.

Japanese professional chefs are often praised for their fancy knife work. Even nonprofessional home cooks in Japan feel comfortable using large, very sharp blades and indulge in decorative cutting and garnishing. The ability to do katsura muki, or broad peel, cutting is often a test of a chef's skill. Slicing chunks of cucumber into broad peels takes a bit of practice, but you'll be well rewarded for your effort.

77

Hold the knife blade at a 45-degree angle to the skin and tug on the skin, using a slight sawing motion; the knife blade shouldn't move. Discard the skin.

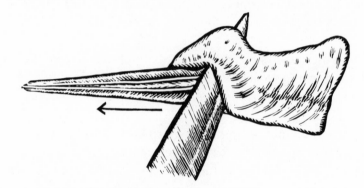

5. Slice the fish across its width into six 1 to 1½-inch-wide paper-thin slices. Slice slightly on the diagonal, much as you would for cutting smoked salmon. (You will roll these slices later so they need to be thin and flexible.) Arrange the slices on the cutting board, and lightly salt the fish to make it ''sweat.'' Rest the board at a slight angle so that any accumulated liquid can run off. Allow the fish to sweat for 5–6 minutes; this improves both texture and flavor.

6. Rinse the cucumber strips in cold water, then gently pat them dry. Rinse off the fish slices in cold water and carefully pat them dry.

7. Assemble the rolls: Lay a strip of cucumber on your cutting board with a short end facing you. Cover two thirds of it with a slice of fish, trimming if necessary to match the fish to the width of the cucumber peels.

8. Drain the red pickled ginger and pat away excess liquid with paper towels (the color may stain cloth). Lay several slivers on the fish across the end nearest you. Snugly roll the cucumber strip to enclose the ginger at the center, and continue to roll, setting it aside with the seam down. Repeat until you have finished rolling all the fish in the cucumber strips; you should have at least six rolls.

9. With scissors, cut six (or more) strips of seaweed. Wind a single band of seaweed around the center of each roll, like a belt. With a sharp knife, slice each roll in half through the center of the seaweed band, to yield 1 dozen (or more) pieces.

10. Stack these circles, two on the bottom and one above in the center, pyramid-style, to make a single portion.

11. Mix the horseradish powder with the cold water to make a thick paste. Coax a bit of this paste into a mound to place beside each stack of fish and cucumber circles. Serve soy sauce on the side; diners dissolve the horseradish in the soy to use as a dipping sauce.

Ocean-Fresh
Sea Bream Arrangement

Kodai no Sashimi

Serves 4

The *sashimi*, or fresh fish, course is an indispensable part of a formal Japanese meal since it characterizes the main tenets of fine Japanese cuisine—impeccably fresh ingredients prepared in an elegant yet unadulterated manner. In this classic presentation, the silky texture and delicate taste of the sea bream is nicely contrasted with a crisp vegetable garnish and a spicy *wasabi*-infused dipping sauce.

> *2 whole very fresh sea bream, each weighing about 12 ounces*

GARNISHES:

> *1 straight unwaxed cucumber, about 6 inches long*
> *1½ inch piece daikon (Japanese white radish)*
> *1½ inch piece carrot, at least 1 inch in diameter*
> *4 edible flowers, optional*
>
> *2 trays of miniature ice cubes (¼-inch cubes or balls)*
> *4 shiso leaves (broad, flat Japanese herb)*

CONDIMENTS:

> *1 tablespoon wasabi (Japanese horseradish) powder*
> *scant tablespoon cold water*
> *soy sauce for dipping*

1. Fillet the fish. Remove the skin from the fillets: Lay a fillet on a clean, dry board, skin side down. Start from the narrow (tail) end and work toward the wider (head) end. Insert the tip of a sharp knife between the skin and the flesh. Hold the knife blade at a 45-degree angle to the skin, and tug on the skin using

a slight sawing motion; the knife blade shouldn't move. Discard the skin.

2. Slice the fish into thin julienne strips. Divide the strips into four portions, and coax each into a mound or tepee-like structure. Cover loosely with clear plastic wrap and refrigerate while you work on the garnishes and presentation.

3. Cut off the stem (darker) end of the cucumber, and rub the cut surface in a circular motion with the sliced-off end piece. A foamy, pasty white substance will appear. This is what the Japanese refer to as *aku*, or bitterness. Rinse it away. Peel the cucumber with a vegetable peeler, if you like, or practice the technique described below to remove the outer skin.

4. Cut the cucumber into 1- to 1½-inch lengths. Using slight up-and-down motions, guide a sharp knife through a cucumber piece to create a long (3 inches or longer), wide, continuous sheet. The Japanese call this kind of cutting *katsura muki*. Discard (or nibble) the core of seeds at the center. Repeat to make at least three unbroken strips.

5. Remove the outer peel from the radish and carrot either with a vegetable peeler or by practicing the *katsura muki* technique. Then cut, *katsura muki* style, at least three unbroken 3-inch-long strips from both the radish and the carrot.

6. Lay the strips of cucumber, radish, and carrot on a board and slice each diagonally into many ¼-inch-wide strips. The strips will curl like ribbon or streamers. Place the strips in a bowl of ice water to crisp them.

7. Fill the bottom of four glass salad bowls or brandy snifters with miniature ice cubes. Rinse the *shiso* leaves in cold water and trim away the stem. Lay a single leaf, smooth side up, on the ice cubes in each bowl. Arrange a mound of fish strips on each green leaf.

8. Mix the horseradish and cold water to make a thick paste. Divide the paste into four portions and coax each into a mound shape. Place a mound of horseradish to the side of each mound of fish.

9. Drain the curlicued vegetables and scatter them across the fish. Further garnish the plates with colorful edible flowers if you like.

10. Each person dissolves as much horseradish as he or she wants in individual dipping dishes containing a few drops of soy sauce; the fish is dipped in the sauce just before you put it in your mouth.

Seared Bonito with Pounded Garlic, Ginger, and Scallions
Katsuo no Tataki

Serves 12–20

If you're a coastal sport fisherman (or have friends who are) and like to barbecue in the summer (or have friends who do), this is the dish for you (and your friends!). In America, bonito is caught off Long Island and along the California coast from May through July. Most of the commercial catch is bought up by local Japanese restaurants, so you may need to find a fishing companion or convince your fish store to special-order it for you. If you can't get bonito, try the same *tataki* preparation with large Spanish mackerel, yellowtail, small bluefin tuna, or Hawaiian mahi mahi (sometimes called dolphin fish).

To make *tataki,* or "pounded," bonito, the fresh fish is filleted, keeping the silvery skin intact. The fillets are then skewered and seared over intense heat to tenderize the skins while keeping the flesh rare and moist. A quick plunge in ice water stops the cooking process while forcing any oils or fats to solidify, facilitating their removal. The lean, rare fish fillets are then patted dry and marinated in a heady combination of soy, ginger, scallions, and garlic before being sliced and served slightly chilled. It is the garlic, scallions, and ginger that are "pounded"—minced, actually—and give the unusual name to this dish.

Bonito, or katsuo *in Japanese, are usually harvested to be processed into dried fillets, which are then shaved into flakes. These* katsuo bushi *flakes are a key ingredient in making traditional stock, and huge quantities are consumed in every Japanese household. Fresh bonito, though, is an early summer delicacy, one that is savored as often as possible in Japan during its short season.*

1 small whole fresh katsuo (*bonito*), *about 6 pounds*
*   ice water*

MARINADE:

½ cup soy sauce

2 tablespoons saké (*Japanese rice wine*)

2 tablespoons rice vinegar

*   juice of 1 small lime, about 2 tablespoons*

2 tablespoons mirin (*syrupy rice wine*)

"POUNDED" CONDIMENTS:

1 tablespoon finely minced fresh ginger

1 large clove garlic, finely minced

2 scallions, finely minced (white and green parts) OR
*   3 tablespoons chopped chives*

GARNISHES (*OPTIONAL*):

10–12 edible flowers such as yellow squash blossoms

1 bunch kaiwaré (*radish sprouts*)

1. Cut off the head of the fish. Trim away the fins. Slit the belly and clean it of all traces of the viscera. Fillet the fish by slicing along the backbone to remove the flesh on both sides of the skeleton; keep the skin intact. Take each fillet and cut it in half lengthwise to remove the center strip of bones and spongy reddish brown flesh. You will have four strips of fish, each about 1 foot long and 2–3 inches wide. Each strip will have skin down the length of one side; the flesh will be about 1 inch thick. Rinse the four strips under cold water and pat dry.

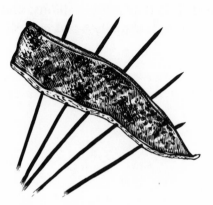

2. Lay one strip of fish, skin side down, on your cutting board and skewer it with five long thin metal skewers (preferably round ones, which are easier to pull out later). Insert the two end skewers first: through the meat just under and parallel to the skin. The two end skewers should form a V in your hands. Now insert a single skewer in the center, then two more skewers on either side of the center one, to form a five-pronged fan. Repeat this skewering process with the remaining three strips of fish.

3. Directly over very high heat, sear the skin for 2–3 minutes. The meat just under the skin will turn white but most of the meat should remain bright red or pink (depending upon the variety of fish); the skin will char and sparks may fly. Twirl the round skewers in place to ensure easy removal later. If the fillet is particularly thick (1½ inches or more), you may want

to sear the flesh side as well: Flip and sear for 1 minute, or until the surface just barely turns color.

4. Plunge the skewered fish into a waiting bowl of ice water to cover. Slide out the skewers. When all the smoke is gone and the fat has floated to the surface, remove the fish from the ice water. Pat the fillet dry. Repeat with the other fillets.

5. Place the fillets on a clean cutting board, charred skin up. With a very sharp knife, slice the fillets into ¼-inch-thick slices; they will be almost triangular in shape, with the skin on one side and meat on the other two. Arrange the slices, leaning up against each other domino-style, in rows on a large ceramic or porcelain platter.

6. In a glass or ceramic bowl, combine the marinade ingredients. Add the minced ginger, garlic, and scallions or chives, and stir. Cover the seared bonito with this mixture, pressing it gently into the fish. Cover the fish with clear plastic wrap and allow it to marinate for 1 hour at room temperature, or for 4–5 hours in the refrigerator.

7. If you want to add a sharp, fresh herbal accent to the dish and have access to edible flowers and/or radish sprouts, rinse them under cold water and shake off excess moisture. Trim away the bottom of the sprouts and scatter them across the fish. Just before serving, scatter the platter with edible flowers.

Small Savories from the Sea

A collection of hot and cold appetizers

Twice-Fried Shrimp Pinecones with Pine Nuts

Ebi no Matsukasa Agé

Makes 1 dozen pieces

The Japanese use a great deal of symbolism in the presentation of their food. Pine trees, for example, represent constant hardiness and are popular motifs in menus celebrating the New Year. These edible pinecones are shaped from a shrimp forcemeat studded with pine nuts and then fried. The forming of these spheres is a bit tricky, but even slightly misshapen, they make delicious hors d'oeuvres!

> 8 ounces uncooked shrimp, shelled and deveined
>
> 1 teaspoon saké (*Japanese rice wine*)
>
> pinch salt
>
> 1 generous tablespoon egg white
>
> 1 tablespoon cornstarch
>
> 2–3 firm white turnips or radishes (*to be used for shaping, not for eating*)
>
> ¼–⅓ cup pine nuts
>
> vegetable oil for deep-frying, at least 2 inches deep
>
> 1 lime, cut into 12 wedges
>
> soy sauce for dipping, optional

1. Chop the shrimp coarsely and then place it in the bowl of a food processor fitted with the steel blade. Pulse/process to finely chop. Add the rice wine and salt, and process until a smooth paste is formed.

2. Combine the egg white with the cornstarch in a small cup, and mix to form a smooth paste. Add the paste to the shrimp mixture, and pulse/process until smooth. Chill, covered, in the refrigerator, at least twenty minutes.

3. Cut twelve rounds from the turnips, each about ¼ inch thick and 1¼ inches in diameter. Stick a single bamboo skewer through each turnip round. These will be used as bases for forming the pinecones.

4. With hands moistened in cold water, divide the shrimp paste into twelve portions, forming each into a rounded oblong shape. Keep the shrimp paste chilled when you are not handling it. Place a single oblong portion of shrimp paste through the skewer so it rests on top of the turnip round. Starting at the base, gently press four or five pine nuts into the shrimp paste. Work your way up the shrimp paste, making four or five rows. Placing the nuts pointing upward gives a more realistic rendering of a pinecone.

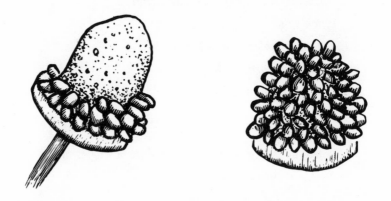

5. Heat the oil in a deep-fryer or wok to about 325 degrees; a pine nut should barely sizzle and color ever so slowly when tested. Holding the exposed portion of the skewer, carefully lower each shrimp pinecone into the hot oil, with the turnip still attached. Gently twirl the skewer to help withdraw it from the center of the shrimp paste. Remove the skewer. Fry only one or two pinecones at a time to keep them from sticking to each other. Fry the shrimp pinecones for 2 minutes, or until fairly firm and slightly golden. Carefully remove them from the oil and drain on paper towels, then slice off the turnip rounds (some may fall off before this point,

which is fine). Repeat until all the pinecones have been fried once. You may find that several pine nuts have fallen off; remove them from the oil and either nibble them on the spot or scatter them over the finished pinecones.

6. Raise the heat of the oil to about 350 degrees, and re-fry the pinecones, three or four at a time, for another 1–1½ minutes. The nuts will become golden and the shrimp paste opaque and firm to the touch. Test for doneness by spearing a pinecone with a toothpick; it should come out clean. Drain the pinecones well on paper towels, and serve them hot or at room temperature with lime wedges. Offer soy sauce for dipping, if you like.

Deep-Fried Seafood Nuggets

Isobé Agé

Makes 24 pieces

Easily as addictive as Cajun-style "popcorn," these bite-size nuggets are made from a mild-tasting fish forcemeat spiced with minced scallion and ginger. The outer wrapping of paper-thin *nori* makes these nuggets crisp and slightly briny while adding to the nutritional value of this snack or hors d'oeuvre.

3 *sheets* yaki nori (*paper-thin toasted seaweed*)

10 *ounces bay* OR *sea scallops*

8 *ounces scrod, pollack, or flounder*

1 *small egg, beaten*

2 *teaspoons* saké (*Japanese rice wine*)

½ *tablespoon finely minced fresh ginger*

1 *tablespoon chopped scallion* (*green part only*)

vegetable oil for deep-frying

soy sauce for dipping, optional

1. Cut each sheet of seaweed into quarters. Then cut each small square in half diagonally, to yield twenty-four small triangles. Set these aside while making the forcemeat.

2. If you are using large sea scallops, cut them in half. Cut the fish into 1-inch pieces. Place the scallops and fish in the bowl of a food processor fitted with the steel blade. Pulse/process to make a rough paste. Add the egg and rice wine, and pulse/process again to make a smooth paste. Add the ginger and scallion greens, and pulse/process to distribute evenly. Carefully transfer the seafood paste to a bowl.

3. Place a rounded teaspoon of seafood paste in the center of each triangle of seaweed. Bring the points of the triangle up and stick them to the paste to form a rounded shape.

4. Heat the oil to about 370 degrees in a deep-fryer or wok. Test with a piece of seaweed: It should sizzle on the surface, turning crisp immediately. Deep-fry the seafood nuggets, about six at a time, for 1 minute. They will puff slightly when frying, and color very lightly. Test with a toothpick if you are unsure; the wooden pick should come out clean, with no fish paste clinging to it.

5. Serve the seafood nuggets hot, with soy sauce on the side for dipping if you wish.

Trout, Southern Barbarian Style

Masu no Namban-Zuké

Serves 4

The "southern barbarians" referred to are the Portuguese and Dutch traders and missionaries who came to Japan in the sixteenth and seventeenth centuries. They showed the Japanese how to deep-fry fish and then pickle it in a spicy vinegar sauce. Any small river or lake fish, such as smelts or minnows, are tasty prepared this way, but I'm particularly fond of trout.

4 very small whole trout, about 3 ounces each, OR *2 whole trout, about 8 ounces each*

¼ *cup cornstarch*

vegetable oil for deep-frying (corn or soy oil with a few drops of dark aromatic sesame oil is best)

PICKLING SAUCE:

⅔ *cup* dashi (*basic sea stock, page 27*)

⅓ *cup rice vinegar*

3 *tablespoons soy sauce*

4 *tablespoons* mirin (*syrupy rice wine*)

3 *tablespoons* saké (*Japanese rice wine*)

1½ *tablespoons sugar*

   pinch salt

1 tōgarashi (*dried red chili pepper*)

GARNISH:

   1 scallion

1. Clean the trout and behead them. Slit and gut the belly cavity. Fillet the fish, trimming off the tail and fins. Rinse the cleaned fish thoroughly. If you are using two large trout, cut each in half to yield four equal-sized pieces from each fish. Gently pat the fish dry on both sides, then dust them with the cornstarch.

2. In a wok or deep-fat fryer, heat the oil to approximately 375 degrees. Test by dropping a pinch of cornstarch in the oil: It should sink ever so slightly, surface, and then disperse immediately, sizzling but not coloring. Deep-fry the pieces of fish, two at a time, for 1½ minutes. With tongs or long cooking chopsticks, turn the fish a few times as you fry them. Drain the fish well on paper towels, and transfer them to a ceramic or glass container just large enough to allow the fish to lie submerged in the pickling sauce.

3. In a small saucepan combine all the pickling sauce ingredients except the dried red pepper. Heat, stirring until the sugar and salt have dissolved. Remove the pan from the heat. Break the pepper pod in half, and discard the seeds if you wish to keep the fish just pleasantly spicy. If your taste runs toward the incendiary, add the seeds as well. Stir the pods (and seeds) into the sauce.

4. Pour the sauce over the fish, and once there is no longer any steam, cover snugly with clear plastic wrap and refrigerate. Pickle the fish for at least 6 hours and up to 72 hours.

(The extended pickling time will "melt" the bones and intensify the piquant taste markedly.)

5. Just before serving, trim the scallion and chop it very finely. Rinse the chopped scallion under cold water to remove any slipperiness and gently squeeze it dry.

6. A single serving is either a half of a larger fish or a whole smaller one. Lift the fish pieces from the pickling sauce and place them on small plates with a rim (to keep the sauce from running). Garnish each portion with a sprinkling of chopped scallion.

Fried Smelts with Bright Mustard Sauce

Kisu no Karashi Miso Soé

Serves 8

Parts of the American Midwest, particularly the Minneapolis–St. Paul region, are known for their spring smelt runs, and batter-frying seems to be the most common way to prepare the abundant catch. Here is a spicy new way to fix the tasty fish, one that the Japanese have been enjoying for centuries.

8 small smelts, about 10–12 ounces

1 teaspoon saké (*Japanese rice wine*)

1 tablespoon soy sauce

1½ tablespoons cornstarch

SAUCE:

⅓ cup shiro miso (*light fermented bean paste*)

1 tablespoon sugar

2 tablespoons rice vinegar

1 teaspoon soy sauce

1 teaspoon hot mustard powder (*preferably* karashi)

1 teaspoon cold water

3–4 tablespoons dashi (*basic sea stock, page 27*)

vegetable oil for deep-frying

1. Prepare the fish for frying: With the back of a knife, scrape off the scales. Remove the heads and trim off the dorsal (back) fins. Slit the belly cavities open to butterfly the fish, and remove the innards. With your fingers, carefully lift the backbones away from the flesh, cutting them off at the tails. Remove the small belly bones too, if you wish, though the Japanese don't usually bother since they are fried very crisp in this dish. Rinse the butterflied fillets under cold water, then pat them dry.

2. Mix the rice wine and soy sauce together, and dip the smelts into the mixture one at a time, making sure that both sides are moistened with the marinade.

3. Pat the fillets dry, and then dust them lightly with the cornstarch. Set the fish aside while making the sauce; the fish will turn a reddish brown as the cornstarch absorbs the soy marinade.

4. Make the bright mustard sauce: In a small glass or enamel-lined double boiler or saucepan, combine the bean paste, sugar, rice vinegar, and soy sauce. Stir with a wooden spoon to mix well, then cook over medium-high heat, stirring, until glossy, bubbly, and slightly thickened (about 1½ minutes). Remove the pan from the heat.

Enjoy this Bright Mustard Sauce with cold poached fish (see the recipe for tilefish on page 144), and with cooked shrimp or clams too.

5. In a small bowl, mix the powdered mustard with the cold water, and stir to make a paste. Add the mustard to the bean sauce, and stir to incorporate well. Thin the sauce with sea stock until it has the consistency of heavy cream.

6. Heat the oil in a deep-fryer or wok to about 370 degrees. Test it with a pinch of cornstarch moistened with soy sauce: It should sizzle on the surface of the oil immediately. Fry the smelts, two at a time, for slightly less than 2 minutes. The fish will be crisp and the oil bubbling around it will become quieter when the fish is cooked. Drain the fish on paper towels. If necessary, fried fish can be kept warm in a preheated 200-degree oven for up to 30 minutes.

7. Serve the fish hot or at room temperature, one per person, napped with the bright mustard sauce as an appetizer or first course.

Spicy Skewered Shrimp

Ebi no Kushi Yaki

You'll be adding these shrimp to your summer barbecue menu often, I'm sure. In Japan they are often added to *obentō* (boxed lunches). You might like to pack these spicy shrimp into your next picnic basket, since they are also delicious cold or at room temperature.

Serves 4–6

> *2 dozen fresh large shrimp, with shells and tails intact*

MARINADE:

> *2 tablespoons* saké (*Japanese rice wine*)

> *2 tablespoons soy sauce*

> *2 tablespoons* mirin (*syrupy rice wine*) OR *½ tablespoon corn syrup*

> *1–2 teaspoons grated fresh ginger*

> *1 slender scallion, finely chopped (white and green parts)*

> *2–3 drops* goma abura (*aromatic sesame oil*) OR rāyu (*hot chili oil*)

> *vegetable oil for the skewers*

1. Rinse the shrimp under cold water and pat them dry. They will be cooked with their shells on to keep them moist. If you want to remove the vein, carefully grasp it at the open end of the shrimp. Straighten out the slight curve of the back of the shrimp as you gently pull out the vein.

2. Combine the marinade ingredients in a glass bowl and soak the shrimp in the mixture, covered, for at least 1 hour at room temperature, or up to 12 hours in the refrigerator.

3. Remove the shrimp from the marinade and thread them on lightly oiled flat metal skewers. Shrimp naturally curve into a "c" shape. Alternate this curve so it opens left and right

The Japanese provide a damp cloth, called an oshibori, at the table or on picnics. It is used to wipe messy fingers. If you'd like to follow their example, use a small washcloth and wet it thoroughly in warm water. Fold the cloth in half and then half again. Roll up the cloth and squeeze it well. The Japanese serve oshibori cloths on bamboo trays, but a small plate stacked with one for each person would be fine, too.

as you skewer the shrimp through the belly section. Place 4–6 shrimp on each skewer.

4. It's best to bring the skewers outdoors and grill them on a barbecue, but if, like me, you enjoy eating these shrimp year-round and you live in a city apartment, you can broil them instead. Preheat your broiler to the highest setting possible. Rest the tips of the skewers on the edges of a disposable foil broiling pan so that the shrimp are suspended in midair, and place them about 1 inch from the source of heat. Broil for 1½ minutes; flip the skewers over and broil for another minute. Brush the shrimp with some of the marinade, and then broil for 1½ more minutes—until the shells become chalky with a bit of charring and the meat is bright pink and opaque.

5. Remove the shrimp from the skewers and serve them hot, in their shells, or let them cool a bit and remove the shells before bringing them to the table.

Mussels Steamed with Ginger

Mūrugai no Shōga Mushi

This recipe was inspired by a recent trip to Seattle, where the tiny Penn Cove mussels that are native to the Pacific Northwest region are among the sweetest, plumpest, loveliest I've tasted! The ginger-steaming method is the genius of Tom Douglas at Cafe Sport, a restaurant at Pike Place Market on Puget Sound. He has been greatly influenced by Japanese technique and presentation, as this recipe shows.

Serves 3–4

3 dozen fresh mussels, preferably small bivalves

2 tōgarashi (*dried red chili peppers*)

6–8 square inches dashi kombu (*kelp for stock making*)

2 tablespoons butter

3 slender scallions, thinly sliced on the diagonal

1 small knob (about ½ ounce) fresh ginger, peeled and cut into fine julienne

¼ cup rice vinegar

¼ cup saké (*Japanese rice wine*)

juice of ½ small lemon

1. Soak the mussels in salty water for 20–30 minutes, to help disgorge any sand. Scrub the mussels well with a brush under cold running water. Remove the "beards."

2. Break the pepper pods in half and discard the seeds, unless you want the mussels to be especially hot.

3. Combine the chili peppers and all the other ingredients in a large wide pot and bring to a boil, covered, over high heat. Add the scrubbed mussels and cover the pot tightly. Steam until the mussels open (you can hear them popping), about 3–3½ minutes.

4. Discard the kelp and pepper pods and serve immediately, with the pot juices poured over the mussels.

Two-Toned Sea Scallops

Hotatégai no Dengaku

Serves 8

In the traditional Japanese kitchen, both light and dark bean pastes are used to make thick *dengaku* sauces; the light bean paste makes a mellow-flavored pale golden sauce, while the dark bean paste makes a more pungent and spicy brown sauce. Seared sea scallops taste delicious topped with both sauces, and here a pair of them—one light and one dark— make a single serving.

16 *large sea scallops*
 1 *tablespoon soy sauce*
 1 *tablespoon* saké (*Japanese rice wine*)
 1 *teaspoon vegetable oil, optional*

MELLOW SAUCE:
 ¼ *cup* shiro miso (*light fermented bean paste*)
 scant 1 tablespoon sugar
 2 *tablespoons* saké (*Japanese rice wine*)

PUNGENT SAUCE:
 ¼ *cup* aka miso (*dark fermented bean paste*)
 2 *tablespoons sugar*
 2 *tablespoons* saké (*Japanese rice wine*)

GARNISHES:
 1 *teaspoon white sesame seeds*
 1 *teaspoon black sesame seeds*

1. Rinse the sea scallops and pat them dry. Lightly score one side of the scallops (to create a less slippery surface on which to spread the sauces).

2. Combine the soy sauce and rice wine, and moisten the scallops in the mixture.

3. Preheat a skillet, add the oil, and sear the scallops in a single layer, scored side first. If you use a non-stick surface, no oil will be necessary. Sear the scallops in batches if necessary. Flip the scallops and cook the other side for 1 minute. Transfer the scallops, scored side up, to a foil-lined rack, pan, or cookie sheet that will fit under your broiler or in your toaster-oven. Set aside, and preheat the broiler.

4. In two small saucepans, combine the ingredients for the mellow sauce and the ingredients for the pungent sauce. Stir each well, and cook them both for 2–3 minutes, stirring as they cook. Both sauces will become glossy, bubbly, and thick, the consistency of ketchup. Set the sauces aside.

5. In a clean, dry skillet, dry-roast the white sesame seeds over high heat for 30–40 seconds. Set them aside in a dish or bowl. Add the black sesame seeds to the same skillet and dry-roast them for 30–40 seconds. Set these aside separately.

6. With a butter knife, spread the scored top of eight scallops with the mellow bean sauce and eight with the pungent bean sauce. Grill the scallops under the broiler for 1 minute, or until bubbly and ever so lightly charred. If you are using a toaster-oven, about 1 minute under top-broil heat should be enough.

7. Garnish the light mellow-sauced scallops with black sesame seeds and the dark pungent-sauced scallops with the white sesame seeds. Serve hot or at room temperature.

Japanese Confetti Omelet

Kani Tamago Yaki

Makes 1 dozen pieces

Japanese cuisine boasts many egg and omelet recipes, often to be served at room temperature or chilled. The bright specks of red ginger, dark mushroom, and green scallion in the yellow omelet give this dish its name. Two pieces of this "confetti" omelet would make a nice first course served alone, especially dramatic on a dark unpatterned plate. This colorful omelet is good for packing along on a picnic, too.

> 6 *large eggs*
>
> 1 *large fresh* shiitaké (*dark oak*) *mushroom, wiped off, stem removed, and cap minced*
>
> 3–4 *ounces fresh crabmeat, picked over and shredded,* OR *imitation crabmeat, well shredded*
>
> 1 *slender scallion, white and green parts finely chopped, each in a separate pile*
>
> *few drops vegetable oil*
>
> 1 *tablespoon* mirin (*syrupy rice wine*)
>
> ¼ *cup* dashi (*basic sea stock, page 27*)
>
> 1½ *teaspoons* usukuchi shōyu (*light soy sauce*)
>
> 1½ *teaspoons finely minced and well drained,* beni shōga (*red pickled ginger*)

1. In a bowl, beat the eggs to thoroughly mix yolk and white, but try not to incorporate air as you do so. Toss the minced mushroom, crabmeat, and the white part of the scallion into the egg mixture. Stir to distribute evenly.

2. Lightly oil a square or rectangular heatproof glass or ceramic dish, or a disposable foil meat-loaf pan measuring about 6 × 8 × 2 inches. (Foil should not be used if you plan to cook the dish in a microwave.)

3. In a small saucepan, combine the syrupy rice wine, sea stock, and light soy sauce. Stir, and bring to a simmer over medium heat.

4. Pour the egg mixture into the simmering seasoned liquid and scramble until very loosely set. Toss in the green part of the scallion and the minced ginger and stir to distribute evenly.

5. Transfer the loosely set omelet mixture to the oiled dish or pan, and smooth the surface with a spatula dipped in cold water.

6. Either steam the omelet over high heat for 3–5 minutes until set, or finish cooking it in a microwave for 1 minute on high setting (full power or 600 watts).

7. Allow the omelet to cool, then chill it slightly. Invert the omelet onto a cutting board to unmold it; there will be some liquid to drain off. Slice the omelet in half lengthwise, then across five times, to yield 1 dozen pieces in all.

Japanese Seafood Terrine
Hampen

Makes 12–16 slices

The Japanese use seafood forcemeat to make a wide variety of dishes such as dumplings, terrines, and stuffings for vegetables. In this recipe, chunks of bright pink shrimp and verdant green asparagus give textural and color contrast to a smooth, snowy fish and seafood terrine. With the help of the food processor and microwave, this terrine is a snap to make.

SURIMI (FORCEMEAT):

> *8–10 ounces bay* OR *sea scallops*
>
> *5–6 ounces turbot* OR *fillet of sole*
>
> *1 tablespoon cornstarch*
>
> *1 tablespoon cold water*
>
> *1 small egg white*
>
> *1 teaspoon* mirin *(syrupy rice wine)*
>
> *1 teaspoon* shiro miso *(light fermented bean paste)*
>
> *¼ teaspoon salt*

> *2–3 stalks fresh green asparagus*
>
> *6 large shrimp*
>
> *1 tablespoon* wasabi *(Japanese horseradish)* powder
>
> *scant 1 tablespoon cold water*
>
> *soy sauce for dipping, optional*

1. Rinse the scallops and pat them dry. If you are using sea scallops, cut them into smaller pieces. Cut the fish into 1-inch pieces. Place the scallops and fish in the bowl of a food processor fitted with the steel blade.

2. Pulse/process the scallops and fish until pasty. Combine the cornstarch and water in a small cup, and mix into a paste. Add the cornstarch paste and pulse/process again. Add the

egg white and process until smooth. Add the bean paste and salt, and pulse/process until well distributed. Transfer the mixture to a bowl.

3. Trim the asparagus and peel the stalks below the tips to remove the triangular "leaves." Cut the asparagus into ¼- to ½-inch pieces. Toss the asparagus pieces into the seafood mixture, and using a spatula, distribute them well.

4. Peel and devein the shrimp, then cut them into ¼- to ½-inch chunks. Toss these into the seafood mixture and distribute them well.

5. Dip a microwave-safe glass loaf pan into cold water, then pour the water out. With hands and/or a rubber spatula dipped in cold water, fill the loaf pan with the seafood mixture. Press gently to make sure there are no air bubbles. Smooth the top of the loaf with a rubber spatula dipped in cold water.

6. Cover the loaf pan with clear plastic wrap. With a toothpick, poke several holes in the plastic wrap to allow steam to escape. Cook the terrine in a microwave oven at medium power (490 watts) for 3 minutes. (Test for doneness by inserting a toothpick in the center of the terrine; it should come out clean.)

7. Let the terrine sit, still wrapped, for 2–3 minutes; it will shrink from the sides of the pan. Remove and discard the plastic wrap, pour off any accumulated liquid, and invert the terrine onto a rack. Cover loosely, and chill it in the refrigerator for at least 30 minutes and up to several hours.

8. When you are ready to serve it, use a sharp knife to slice the terrine. Mix the horseradish powder with the cold water to make a paste. Place small mounds of the paste to the side of one or two slices of terrine on each plate. Serve soy sauce on the side for dipping, if you like.

Lemon-Simmered Clams with Herbs

Hamaguri no Remon Ni

Serves 2–3

Simmering steamed clams in their own broth spiked with fresh lemon juice gives them an intense flavor—rich and briny with sunny citrus overtones. An added bonus is the way these clams keep for hours at room temperature, making them great for a picnic as well as a buffet.

> *2 dozen hard-shell or quahog clams*
>
> *6–8 square inches* dashi kombu (*kelp for stock making*)
>
> *3 tablespoons* saké (*Japanese rice wine*)
>
> *3 tablespoons fresh lemon juice*
>
> *1 teaspoon soy sauce*
>
> *½ lemon, cut into very thin rounds*
>
> *1 tablespoon* ao nori (*sea herb flakes*)
>
> *1 tablespoon finely minced parsley*

1. Scrub the clams and soak them in salted water for 20–30 minutes to help disgorge any sand.

2. Place the clams in a wide-mouthed pot with the kelp, rice wine, and lemon juice. Cover the pot, place it over high heat, and steam open the clams (about 2½ minutes). Discard any that don't open after 3 or 4 minutes.

3. Discard the kelp and strain the broth into a skillet. Season the steaming broth with the soy sauce, and bring it to a boil over high heat; then adjust the heat to maintain a low boil.

4. Remove the clam meats from their shells and add them to the bubbling broth. Simmer the clams for 8–10 minutes,

turning them occasionally, until the broth is nearly gone. Allow the clams to cool to room temperature in the skillet.

5. Arrange the lemon slices in a circle on a serving platter, and mound the simmered clams on the lemon slices. Mix the sea herb flakes with the minced parsley, and sprinkle the mixture over the clams.

Soy-Simmered Conch

Sazaé no Shōyu Ni

Serves 4–6

The Japanese steam and simmer all manner of molluscs, then cool them and thinly slice the meat to serve as chewy snacks with icy beer in the hot weather, or with warmed *saké* in the chilly months. Although the Japanese favor an abalone-like creature called *tokubushi* for this kind of soy simmering,

the most readily available single-shelled mollusc in America is conch, also known as whelk. They are sold here as presteamed steaks. In the Pacific Northwest, geoduck is sometimes available, and is delicious when prepared *shōyu ni* style.

3–4 *presteamed conch steaks about 2 ounces each* OR
    2 *live geoduck clams about 4 ounces each*

1–2 *cups water*

  2 *tablespoons* saké (*Japanese rice wine*)

  1 *tablespoon sugar*

3–4 *tablespoons soy sauce*

1. If you are using presteamed conch steaks, blanch them in boiling water to barely cover for 2 minutes. Drain, and proceed to step 3.

2. If you are using geoduck clams, immerse them in rapidly boiling water for 30 seconds, then transfer them to a bowl of ice water. The hot "bath" should have loosened the skin from the siphon meat (the part extending from the shell) and from the shell. Remove the skin from the siphon meat and cut off this portion, which requires longer cooking than the belly meat. Discard the shell, and trim the viscera away from the belly meat. Parboil the siphon meat for 15–20 minutes in water to barely cover (add more water only as necessary to keep the meat from scorching). Add the belly meat to the pot and cook for another 5–6 minutes. Strain the broth and reserve it separately from meat.

3. Place the conch steaks or geoduck siphon and belly meats in either water or broth (reserved from parboiling) to cover. Add the rice wine and bring to a boil. Skim away any froth, adjust the heat to maintain a low boil, and cook for 3–4 minutes. (Throughout the simmering process, it is best to use an *otoshi-buta*, or dropped lid, described here. If you do not have a dropped lid, remember to baste the simmering meats often with the seasoned liquid.)

4. Add the sugar and continue to cook for another 3–4 minutes. If the conch or geoduck looks to be in danger of scorching, add a few drops more water or broth.

5. Add the soy sauce and continue to cook for 5–6 minutes, or until nearly all the liquid is gone and the meat is slightly glazed. Allow the conch or geoduck to cool to room temperature in the cooking pot.

6. Before serving, slice the conch or clam meats into thin (1/16-inch) slices. Arrange individual portions of 5–6 slices, leaning against each other domino-style, on small plates.

7. If you want to make a large amount of soy-simmered conch or clam meats to keep for another occasion, store them whole. Wrapped in clear plastic wrap and refrigerated, the meats will keep for a week to 10 days.

An otoshi-buta *or "dropped lid" is found in nearly every Japanese kitchen. Made from a cedar-like wood, it is slightly smaller than the circumference of the pot in which it is used. Instead of resting on the rim of the pot, the lid rests directly on the food inside. Particularly useful when simmering or braising with just a bit of liquid, it keeps the food moist while allowing the liquid to reduce and intensify slowly. The bubbling liquid hits against the inside of the lid during the cooking process and flavors and colors the top surfaces of the food as well as the bottom. Sold in many Oriental groceries throughout America, buy a size 1/2–1 inch smaller than the diameter of your pot. Since the lids are made of wood, it is best to wash them with mild soap and warm water and let them dry naturally.*

Mussels with Mustard Sauce and Scallions

Mūrugai no Karashi Miso Aé

Serves 2–3

This is a classic appetizer in Japan, where it is served from late winter through early spring and again in the autumn. On warm days it's served with a frosty glass of cold beer; on chilly days it's best with warmed *saké*.

> *2 dozen mussels*
> *6–8 square inches* dashi kombu (*kelp for stock making*)
> *¼ cup* saké (*Japanese rice wine*)

MUSTARD SAUCE:

> *3 tablespoons* shiro miso (*light fermented bean paste*)
> *2 tablespoons sugar*
> *1½ teaspoons rice vinegar*
> *1½ teaspoons* karashi (*hot Japanese mustard*) *powder*

> *4–5 slender scallions with pretty green tops*

1. Soak the mussels in salted water to cover for 20–30 minutes to help disgorge any sand. Scrub the mussels and remove their beards.

2. Place the mussels in a wide-mouthed pot. Add the kelp and wine, cover, and cook over high heat until the mussels open, about 3 minutes. Discard any unopened mussels after 4 or 5 minutes. Strain the broth through a cloth- or paper-lined strainer and reserve it. Remove the mussel meats from their shells and let them cool in the reserved broth while you make the mustard sauce.

3. Combine the bean paste, sugar, and 1 tablespoon of the reserved mussel broth in a small saucepan. Stir to combine

well. Cook the sauce over medium heat, stirring, until bubbly and glossy, about 2 minutes. Remove the sauce from the heat. Combine the vinegar and mustard powder to make a paste, and stir this into the sauce.

4. Trim the scallions and cut them into ¾-inch lengths. In a small saucepan, blanch them in boiling water to cover for 20 seconds, just long enough to wilt them yet keep the color vivid. Drain and rinse under cold water. Gently press out all excess liquid from the scallions.

5. The sauce, mussels, and scallions can all be chilled separately at this point if you wish to serve this dish more than 30 minutes later. Just before serving, remove the mussel meats from their broth and combine them with the blanched scallions. If the mustard sauce seems very thick (like tomato paste rather than yogurt), or if you want to intensify the mussel flavor, thin the sauce slightly with a few drops of mussel broth. Toss the mussels and scallions in the mustard sauce to mix well. Serve them warm or at room temperature in small individual mounds.

Red and White Half-Moons
Kōhaku Kasané

Serves 6–8

Silky smoked salmon pairs with crisp tart white radish to form half-moon shapes. These make a stunning accompaniment to any grilled or fried entrée.

SWEET-AND-SOUR SAUCE:

½ cup vinegar

3 tablespoons sugar

½ teaspoon salt

4 inch length daikon (*Japanese white radish*), *at least 2 inches in diameter*

pinch salt

4 ounces sliced smoked salmon

1 bunch kaiwaré (*radish sprouts*), OR *4 sprigs of watercress*

1. Combine the sweet-and-sour sauce ingredients in a small glass or enamel-lined saucepan. Cook over moderate heat, stirring, to dissolve the salt and sugar. Let the sauce cool.

2. Peel the radish, then slice it into thin (¹⁄₁₆-inch) rounds. Lay the rounds out on a cutting board and sprinkle them with the salt. With your fingertips, gently rub the salt into the radish slices. Let the slices sit for a few moments, then rinse them in cold water. Pat the slices dry, then place them in the cooked sauce. Let the slices marinate for at least 15 minutes at room temperature, or up to 24 hours covered and refrigerated.

3. Lift the radish slices from the sauce and pat away any excess liquid. Lay a single slice on your cutting board. Lay a slice of smoked salmon on top to cover it; cut and trim the

salmon as necessary to achieve an even layer. Top with another slice of radish; gently press the "sandwich" together. Repeat, making as many sandwiches as you can from the radish and salmon slices. Line up the sandwiches on your cutting board, cover them with clear plastic wrap, and place another cutting board on top to weigh down the sandwiches. Refrigerate for at least 10 minutes and up to 12 hours.

4. Remove the top cutting board and slice each sandwich in half. Arrange three or four of these, leaning against each other domino-style, to make a single portion.

5. Rinse the radish sprouts under cold water, shake off excess moisture, and trim away the stems. Or rinse and trim the sprigs of watercress. Garnish each serving of Red and White Half-Moons with some radish sprouts or a sprig of watercress.

 115

Sea Urchin Roe in Amber
Uni no Kanten

Makes 3 dozen bite-size pieces

Fresh sea urchin roe is a costly delicacy in Japan and most often adorns individual nuggets of *sushi*. Here, chunks of the roe are suspended in an amber-colored aspic to make a more economical yet equally delicious appetizer. For those who love the delicate, briny taste of sea urchin, these jewel-like pieces make a spectacular addition to any tray of hors d'oeuvres.

The classic recipe in Japan calls for *kanten* (agar-agar), which is processed from sea vegetables, not animal protein, and jells more firmly than conventional gelatin. For those who prefer a softer texture, 1 envelope (2 teaspoons) of ordinary gelatin is a fine substitute.

> *1 stick* kanten (*Japanese agar-agar gelatin*), OR
>   *1 envelope (4 grams) powdered* kanten
>
> *1 cup* Tosa dashi (*smoky sea stock, page 28*)
>
> *2 tablespoons* saké (*Japanese rice wine*)
>
> *2 tablespoons sugar*
>
> *4 tablespoons soy sauce*
>
> *1 tablespoon chopped fresh chives*
>
> *2–3 pieces (about 1 ounce)* uni (*sea urchin roe*)

1. Break the stick of *kanten* into several pieces and soak them in cold water to cover for at least 10 minutes. If you are using powdered *kanten*, sprinkle it over 2 tablespoons cold water and let it stand for at least 5 minutes before you use it.

2. In a saucepan, combine the smoky sea stock, rice wine, sugar, and soy sauce. Bring to a simmer and cook for 2 minutes. Add water if necessary to make 1¾ cups liquid.

3. Squeeze out all the water from the pieces of *kanten*, and with your hands shred the softened mass into the saucepan

containing the seasoned stock. Or add the softened powdered *kanten*. Cook the mixture over low heat, stirring constantly, until the *kanten* dissolves completely (this could take as long as 10 minutes). Simmer for 2–3 minutes longer.

4. Pour a few drops of the liquid *kanten* into the bottom of thirty-six small ruffly foil cups (about ¾-inch diameter). It will jell quickly, so immediately sprinkle a few bits of chive in each cup, before the *kanten* sets.

5. Cut the sea urchin roe into thirty-six chunks, each less than ½ inch. Place a single piece in each of the *kanten*-filled cups. Sprinkle the top of each piece of roe with some more of the chives. Carefully ladle in the remaining amber-colored liquid (if it has jelled, reheat slowly to dissolve), to fill each cup close to the brim. If any bubbles have formed, drag them to the sides of the foil cup with the tip of a toothpick, either lancing the bubbles or pulling them up the sides of the foil. The aspic will harden quickly without chilling, though refrigeration will hasten this along. Once all steam is gone and the aspic is firm, cover and chill for at least 1 hour, or up to 4 days.

6. Serve the roe-in-amber either in the original foil cups, or peel the cups away and invert.

Oysters on the Half Shell with Spicy Sauce

Kaki no Momiji Kaké

Serves 2–3

The tiny Olympia oysters harvested off the Seattle coast are perhaps the sweetest, most succulent oysters I've ever had. One evening at Ray's Boathouse, a well-known local fish and seafood restaurant, I had a platter of them with a wonderfully spicy sauce that reminded me of the Japanese *momiji* ("autumn leaves") sauce, so named because of its burnished red color. The sauce can be made anywhere you can find fresh Japanese white radish, and I suggest you buy whatever local oysters are freshest and best.

"MAPLE LEAF" SAUCE:

⅓ *cup rice vinegar*

1 *teaspoon soy sauce (preferably* usukuchi shōyu, *or light soy sauce)*

pinch salt

1½ *teaspoons sugar*

7–8 *ounces* daikon (*Japanese white radish*), *about 8 inches long and 1½ inches in diameter*

½ *teaspoon* ichimi tōgarashi (*powdered red chili pepper*)

3 *dozen tiny fresh oysters,* OR *fewer large oysters*

1. In a small saucepan, combine the vinegar, soy sauce, salt, and sugar. Heat through (about 1 minute), stirring, to dissolve the sugar and salt. Transfer the sauce to a glass jar and refrigerate while you grate the radish.

2. Peel the radish and grate it on the finest grater setting you can. Squeeze the gratings gently and pour off the excess

liquid. Combine the radish with the chili pepper powder, and stir to distribute well. Add enough of the vinegar sauce to moisten the radish but not so much that it is thin and runny. (Leftover sauce can be used as a dipping sauce for cooked shrimp or clams. It can also be transferred to a lidded glass jar and refrigerated for several weeks.)

3. Shuck the oysters and serve them on the half shell with the sauce spooned over them. If you like, cover and chill the oysters and sauce separately for 1 hour before serving, assembling them at the last minute.

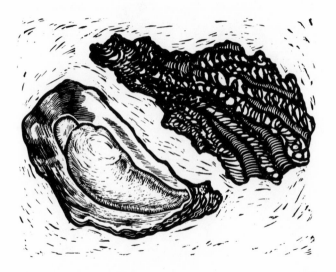

Salads from the Sea

A few seafood and vegetable combinations dressed in sprightly sauces and dressings—several to be served as appetizers, others to be enjoyed as light entrées

Crabmeat, Cucumber, and Radish Salad

Kani to Kyūri no Sunomono

Serves 4

A few tart mouthfuls of seafood and crisp vegetables are often served with other grilled, fried, or steamed entrées in Japan.

5–6 ounces fresh crab lumpmeat OR imitation crab legs

3–4 blemish-free red radishes

1 slender unwaxed cucumber, about 4 inches long

TART DRESSING:

¼ cup rice vinegar

1 tablespoon usukuchi shōyu (light soy sauce)

1 teaspoon mirin (syrupy rice wine)

1. Pick over the crabmeat to remove all traces of cartilage, or cut the imitation crab legs into ½-inch lengths and flake the meat.

2. Trim off the top and bottom of each radish, then slice them into paper-thin circles. Stack several of these circles on each other and slice them into thin thread-like julienne strips. The strips will be white, tipped with bright red. Soak the radish strips in cold water for a few minutes to help crisp them.

3. Trim off the stem (darker) end of the cucumber, and rub the cut ends together with a circular motion. A white pasty substance will form around the edge. The Japanese call this *aku*, or bitterness. Rinse this *aku* off and pat the cucumber dry. Trim off the other end, then cut the cucumber in half to make two cylinders, each about 2 inches long. Each cylinder will be decoratively cut to yield two "mountains." Insert the

point of a small, sharp knife lengthwise through the middle of one of the cucumber pieces. Keep that knife in place while using a second knife to slash the cucumber on the diagonal. Keeping the first knife in place, flip the cucumber cylinder over and with the second knife make another diagonal slash in the same direction. Remove both knives and pull the cucumber "mountains" apart. Repeat with the other cylinder to make four mountains in all.

4. In a small bowl, combine the dressing ingredients. Toss the flaked crabmeat in the dressing and allow it to sit for 10–15

minutes. Then, pressing gently against the crabmeat, pour off and reserve the excess dressing.

5. Drain the radish shreds and toss them in the excess dressing. Allow the radish to sit in the dressing for 5–10 minutes, then drain off the excess.

6. In each of four glass salad bowls or large brandy snifters, arrange a single green cucumber mountain to the left and toward the back. Divide the crabmeat into four portions, and mound each portion slightly in front and to the right of the cucumber mountain. Divide the radish shreds into four portions and scatter them on top of each portion of crab. Cover and chill for 10 minutes (or for up to 2 hours) before serving.

Squid and Endive Salad with Ginger Vinaigrette

Ika no Shōga Su Aé

Serves 3–4 as an appetizer

Several varieties of squid and cuttlefish are regularly available throughout the year in Japan. In the colder months *mongō ika,* or giant thick-fleshed cuttlefish, appears on many menus and tables, while in the spring and summer, slender, petite *yari ika* is at its best. This dish is fine made with either variety—the thicker cuttlefish can be cut into highly decorative curlicues; the thinner squid is best cut into julienne strips.

DRESSING:

- ⅓ *cup rice vinegar*
- 1½ *tablespoons sugar*
- ½ *teaspoon salt*
- ½ *teaspoon* usukuchi shōyu (*light soy sauce*)
- 1 *teaspoon ginger juice* (*extracted from grated fresh ginger*)

- 4 *small squid, about 3 ounces each,* OR *1 large block frozen cleaned cuttlefish, about 10–12 ounces* (*see step 2*)
- 2 *teaspoons* saké (*Japanese rice wine*)
- 1 *small head Belgian endive*
- 1 *small head radicchio lettuce*

1. In a small saucepan, combine the vinegar, sugar, salt, and light soy sauce. Heat it over a low flame, stirring, until the sugar and salt have completely dissolved. Cool the mixture to room temperature, then add the ginger juice and stir.

2. The thick-fleshed cuttlefish is usually sold frozen as already cleaned blocks of *sashimi* quality; defrost it in the refrigerator overnight.

If you buy whole small squid, either have the fishmarket clean them for you or do it yourself: Pull the sac with legs attached out and away from the body. Slice away and discard the sac, reserving the legs if you like for use in either Lacy Seafood Pancakes (page 162) or Broth with Squid and Vegetables (page 40). Pull the "quill" out from the body of the squid and discard. Repeat to clean all the squid.

3. Slit the bodies of the small squid so they can lie flat in a triangular configuration. The inner surface (the one with the ridges from where the "quill" used to be) should be facing down on your cutting board. Slice the squid on the diagonal into ⅛-inch-thick strips.

If you are using the thick-fleshed cuttlefish, add a decorative pattern to the snowy white flesh: Holding a very sharp long-bladed knife at a 45-degree angle to the cuttlefish, slash it in many diagonal strokes. Then cut the cuttlefish into strips on the diagonal in the opposite direction of the slashes, so that they will later open up and create attractive curlicue forms.

Toss the squid or cuttlefish strips in 1 teaspoon of the rice wine.

4. Bring a saucepan of water to a rolling boil and add the other teaspoon of rice wine to it. Drop the squid or cuttlefish strips into the water, stirring to keep them from sticking to each other. Blanch the squid for 45 seconds or until the water

returns to a boil, whichever comes first. Blanch the cuttlefish for 10 seconds after the water returns to a boil. *Do not overcook the squid or cuttlefish.* Drain the squid or cuttlefish immediately and toss it in the dressing. Chill for 5–10 minutes.

5. Cut the endive into thin julienne strips. Toss these into the dressing with the squid, and mix well. Trim and rinse the radicchio leaves.

6. To assemble the salad, place radicchio leaves on each of three or four plates. Divide the squid and endive into three or four portions, and mound it on the leaves.

Ocean Salad with Lemon-*Miso* Dressing

Kaisō Sarada

Serves 4

Some sea vegetables are harvested by season, just like corn or pumpkins. *Wakamé*, or sea-tangle, is sweetest and most lustrous in the early spring, and that's when it's harvested in Japan. At that time *wakamé* is sometimes served fresh, as *sashimi*, although most of the crop is dried and stored for the year to come. This salad uses dried *wakamé* since it is readily available in specialty stores.

The recipe here offers two dressings, one that is classic, the other contemporary. Both owe their tart, robust flavor to a lemon and *miso* (bean paste) mixture; the traditional dressing is thick like a sauce, while the modern one, based on a Continental-type vinaigrette, pours easily. The *miso* vinaigrette dressing is also fabulous on tossed greens.

> *1 small daikon (Japanese white radish), about 12 ounces*
> *¼ teaspoon salt*
> *1 large carrot, about 5 ounces*
> *1 packet (5 grams) dried cut wakamé (sea-tangle)*

CLASSIC LEMON-*MISO* SAUCE:
> *¼ cup shiro miso (light fermented bean paste)*
> *1 tablespoon sugar*
> *2 tablespoons fresh lemon juice*
> *½ teaspoon grated lemon peel*

VINAIGRETTE DRESSING, OPTIONAL:
> *1½ tablespoons rice vinegar*
> *3 tablespoons water*
> *2 tablespoons fruity olive oil*

1. Peel the radish, then cut it into fine thread-like julienne strips about 1½ inches long. Place these in a bowl and sprinkle with half the salt.

2. Peel the carrot, and cut it into 1½-inch-long segments. Cut the carrot into fine thread-like julienne strips. Place these in a separate bowl and sprinkle with the remaining salt.

3. Soak the sea-tangle in the water for 10 minutes.

4. In a small saucepan, mix the bean paste with the sugar and lemon juice. Stirring, cook over medium heat for 2–3 minutes, until glossy, bubbly, and thick. Remove the pan from the heat and stir in the grated lemon peel. Allow the sauce to cool to room temperature.

If you wish, combine the vinaigrette dressing ingredients in a glass jar with a tight-fitting lid. Add the classic sauce while it is still warm, cover, and shake to mix the dressing. Chill the dressing. (Just before using, shake again.)

5. Squeeze the shredded radish to wilt it, and pour away the accumulated liquid. Rinse the radish under cold water to remove all traces of salt. Squeeze and/or spin dry. Follow the same procedure for the carrot shreds.

6. Drain the sea-tangle, blotting away excess moisture with paper towels.

7. In each of four glass bowls, mound a portion of the shredded radish, the shredded carrot, and the green sea-tangle. Chill, or serve at room temperature.

8. Either place a dollop of traditional sauce to the side of the mounded vegetables, or drizzle the contemporary *miso* vinaigrette lightly over the vegetables.

Smoked Whitefish Salad with Plum Dressing

Masu no Bainiku Aé

Serves 4

The Japanese typically serve smoked fish in small boneless, skinless chunks, with a dollop of thick plum sauce to the side. Here I've combined a traditional sweet-and-sour plum sauce with a light vinaigrette, making a tart dressing to nap the rich flaked fish. I've set out a generous mound of the fish salad on soft lettuce; you might want to serve it with bread sticks or rolls for brunch.

   1 pound smoked whitefish

TRADITIONAL PLUM SAUCE:

   3 tablespoons bainiku OR neri umé (*both mean "pickled plum paste"*)

   1 tablespoon shiro miso (*light fermented bean paste*)

   1½ teaspoons mirin (*syrupy rice wine*)

   1 teaspoon dashi (*basic sea stock, page 27*) OR *water*

SALAD DRESSING:

   1 tablespoon vegetable oil

   2 teaspoons rice vinegar

   1 teaspoon water

   1 head Boston OR Bibb lettuce

1. Remove the skin from the whitefish and break the flesh into small chunks. Flake the fish, being sure to remove all small bones as you do. Set the flaked fish aside in a bowl.

2. In a small saucepan, combine the traditional plum sauce ingredients. Stir until smooth, and cook over low heat for 2–3 minutes, until bubbly, glossy, and fragrant. Stir occasionally as you cook. (Remove the saucepan from the heat and let the sauce cool to room temperature if you want to use it plain, or store it in a glass jar in the refrigerator for some future use.)

3. In a glass jar or bottle with a tight-fitting lid, mix the salad dressing ingredients. Shake to distribute. Add the warm plum sauce, and shake to make a thick dressing.

4. Pour half the dressing over the flaked fish, and toss to incorporate well. Chill both the dressed fish and the remaining dressing, separately.

5. Wash and spin-dry the lettuce. Divide the leaves among four plates, and arrange a mound of dressed fish in the center of each plate. Serve additional plum dressing on the side.

Shrimp and Avocado Salad with Ginger-Soy Dressing, A la Shinozawa

Ebi no Shōga-Jōyu Doresshingu

Serves 4

Many Japanese restaurants in the United States serve a small green salad with a soy-based dressing, and their happy American patrons are convinced that it is a "classic" Japanese dish. It's not classic, though it is authentic. The soy-based vinaigrette is a popular dressing served with main-course seafood salads at many Continental-style restaurants in Japan. The following recipe comes compliments of Chef Shinozawa of the Blue Gardenia restaurant, atop the forty-story Akasaka Prince Hotel in Tokyo.

> 2 dozen large shrimp with shells and tails intact
>
> 2 tablespoons saké (*Japanese rice wine*)
>
> 1 tablespoon cornstarch
>
> 1 packet (*about 5 ounces*) harusamé (*"spring rain"*) noodles
>
> 1 large, very ripe avocado
>
> 1–2 tablespoons fresh lemon juice

SHINOZAWA DRESSING:

3 tablespoons fruity olive oil

1 tablespoon soy sauce

2 tablespoons rice vinegar

1 teaspoon fresh orange juice

1 teaspoon fresh lemon juice

1 teaspoon very finely minced fresh ginger

1 teaspoon very finely minced onion

½ teaspoon grated orange and/or lemon peel, optional

   pinch salt

   pinch freshly ground black pepper

1 head Boston OR other soft-leafed lettuce, separated, washed, and spun dry

1. Peel the shrimp, leaving the tail and last segment of shell attached. With a sharp knife, make a shallow slit down the rounded back of each shrimp and devein it.

2. Mix the rice wine and cornstarch until smooth. Toss the shrimp in the mixture to coat them well. Bring a small pot of water to a rolling boil and blanch the shrimp, five or six at a time, for 1 minute until just tender. Remove the shrimp from the pot with a slotted spoon and let them cool to room temperature. Then cover them with clear plastic wrap, and chill them.

3. Bring a fresh pot of water to a boil and cook the noodles for 1 minute. Remove the pot from the heat, and let the noodles soak in the hot water for another 3–5 minutes. Drain, rinse under cold water to remove excess starch, and drain again. Cover, and chill the noodles until ready to serve.

4. Slice the avocado into eight strips; peel off the skin and cut each strip into thirds, slightly on the diagonal. Toss these pieces in the lemon juice, to hold their color. Cover, and chill until ready to serve.

5. Combine the dressing ingredients in a blender, and process until the mixture is smooth and all ingredients are well distributed. Add the citrus peel for extra texture and a refreshingly bitter "bite."

6. Assemble the plates: On each of four dinner plates, arrange lettuce leaves to cover most of the center surface. Arrange six shrimp on the lettuce toward the left and back; mound a portion of the avocado pieces to the right of the shrimp. Divide the noodles into four portions, and arrange one in the front center position of each plate. Serve the dressing separately for everyone to pour over their salad.

Halibut Salad with Citron Dressing

Ohyō no Yuzu-Miso Aé

Serves 3–4 as a main course, 6 as a first course

Japanese citron, or *yuzu*, adds a delightful flavor and aroma to many dishes in its native land. Here, the pure white, delicate flesh of poached halibut is beautifully paired with a *yuzu*-based dressing. The essence of this fruit's peel is sold in small glass vials in many Oriental markets in the United States, and its unique flavor and aroma make it well worth the trouble of tracking this ingredient down. But if your best efforts at obtaining *yuzu* essence remain unrewarded, know that the alternative lemon-lime dressing is also marvelous.

12–14 ounces halibut (the less expensive tail piece is perfect)

POACHING LIQUID:

   6–8 square inches dashi kombu (*kelp for stock making*)

   2–3 thin slices fresh lemon

   ¼ cup saké (*Japanese rice wine*)

   1 cup water

CITRON DRESSING:

   1½ tablespoons shiro miso (*light fermented bean paste*)

   1 teaspoon yuzu *essence*

   ½ teaspoon mirin (*syrupy rice wine*)

   1 teaspoon strained broth from poaching

ALTERNATE LEMON-LIME DRESSING:

   2 tablespoons shiro miso (*light fermented bean paste*)

   1 teaspoon fresh lemon juice

   1 teaspoon fresh lime juice

   ½ teaspoon grated lemon peel

   ½ teaspoon mirin (*syrupy rice wine*)

   small bunch watercress (about 1 dozen sprigs)

1. Place the fish in a pot just large enough to hold it comfortably. Add the poaching liquid ingredients and cover. Bring to a simmer over medium heat, then reduce the heat to maintain a gentle but steady simmer. Poach the fish, covered, for 5–6 minutes after the liquid has begun to bubble. Remove the pot, still covered, from the stove and let the fish sit in the hot liquid for 10–15 minutes. When you can comfortably handle the fish, remove it from the pot. Strain a bit of poaching liquid to reserve for later use.

2. Remove the skin and bones from the fish. Flake the meat into fairly large chunks. Cover, and refrigerate while making the dressing.

3. In a bowl, combine the citron or lemon-lime dressing ingredients, stirring to blend well. Toss the fish with the dressing, cover, and refrigerate again. Chill for at least 30 minutes or up to 12 hours.

4. Reserve several of the prettiest sprigs of watercress for garnishing the salad. Finely mince the remaining watercress; there should be about 2 tablespoons. Just before serving, toss the minced watercress with the fish.

5. The Japanese would serve small individual mounds of this sauced fish with a sprig of watercress jauntily leaning against it. You may prefer to place the salad on a bed of lettuce, or serve it spread on crackers or bread.

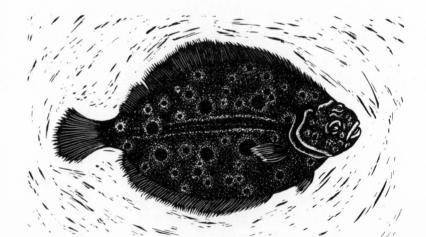

In the Mainstream

Hot and cold main-course dishes, prepared in a variety of ways: poached and chilled, deep-fried, steamed, broiled and skillet-glazed, and simmered

TO BE STEAMED

TO BE BROILED, GRILLED, OR SKILLET-GLAZED

TO BE POACHED OR SIMMERED

Cold Poached Salmon with Sweet-and-Sour Yellow Sauce

Shaké no Kimizu Aé

Serves 3–4

On a hot summer day, this salmon dish will be very much appreciated. The bright yellow sauce is just tart enough to awaken your taste buds yet rich enough to satisfy your hunger. It comes as a surprise to many Westerners to learn that several egg-thickened sauces, such as this one, are part of traditional Japanese cuisine. In Japan, this sweet-and-sour sauce is served with a variety of cooked fish and shellfish.

1 fillet of salmon, about 14 ounces

¼ teaspoon salt

POACHING BROTH:

15–20 square inches dashi kombu (kelp for stock making)

2 cups cold water

1 tablespoon saké (Japanese rice wine)

1 slice lemon

SAUCE:

1 teaspoon sugar

¼ teaspoon salt

¼ cup rice vinegar

1 jumbo egg yolk

2–3 tablespoons dashi (basic sea stock, page 27) OR water

1. Lay a double thickness of cheesecloth on a cutting board. Place the salmon fillet, skin side down, on the cheesecloth.

Check to be sure all bones have been removed along the center line of the fillet. Lightly salt the fish. Fold over the ends of the cheesecloth to enclose the fish.

2. Prepare the poaching broth: In a fish poacher, combine the kelp and cold water and bring the water to a boil. Remove from the heat, season with the rice wine, and add the slice of lemon.

3. Carefully place the wrapped salmon in the poaching broth, skin side down. Arrange the kelp so that it rests on top of the fish, almost like an inner lid. Over low heat, poach the salmon 10–12 minutes. Ladle the poaching liquid over the kelp and fish frequently.

4. Remove the pot from the heat, and allow the fish to cool in the poaching broth. Then remove the salmon from the broth and chill it, still wrapped in cheesecloth and covered with kelp, in the refrigerator for at least 1 hour and up to 12 hours.

5. In a small saucepan combine the sugar, salt, and vinegar. Over low heat, stirring, cook the mixture about 1 minute until the sugar and salt have dissolved. Chill this mixture for at

least 1 hour. Then add the egg yolk to the chilled vinegar mixture, and stir with a wooden spoon or paddle until smooth. Place the mixture over a double boiler and cook the sauce, stirring, until thickened, like a custard. If the sauce should curdle, it can be smoothed by forcing it through a fine-meshed sieve and mixing in a few drops of stock or water. Chill the sauce. Just before using it, thin the sauce to the consistency of heavy cream by stirring in the stock or water, a few drops at a time.

6. Slice the poached salmon into three or four pieces and serve, skin side down, with sauce spooned over the pink flesh.

Cold Poached Tilefish with Mustard-*Miso* Sauce and Fiddleheads

Sakana no Karashi Miso An Kaké, Kogomi Soé

Serves 3–4

Here is another poached fish dish, perfect for a warm-weather menu. The mustard adds zing to an otherwise mellow sauce. The Japanese often serve this poached and sauced fish in the spring, when edible fronds and bracken such as *warabi* and *kogomi* are in season. Lately fiddlehead fern fronds have appeared in American markets, and they would be lovely served with the fish—as would barely blanched fresh green asparagus, if you can't find the more exotic fiddleheads.

> *1 large fillet of tilefish, about 14 ounces*
> *¼ teaspoon salt*

POACHING BROTH:

> *15–20 square inches* dashi kombu (*kelp for stock making*)
> *2 cups cold water*
> *1 tablespoon* saké (*Japanese rice wine*)

> *½ pound fresh* kogomi (*fiddlehead fern fronds*)
> *pinch* yakimyōban (*alum*), *optional*

MUSTARD SAUCE:

> *⅓ cup* shiro miso (*light fermented bean paste*)
> *1 tablespoon sugar*
> *1 teaspoon soy sauce*
> *2 tablespoons rice vinegar*
> *1 teaspoon* karashi (*hot Japanese mustard powder*)
> *mixed with 1 scant teaspoon cold water to make a paste*
> *2–3 tablespoons* dashi (*basic sea stock, page 27*) OR *water*

1. Lay a double thickness of cheesecloth on a cutting board. Place the tilefish fillet, skin side down, on the cheesecloth. Check to be sure all bones have been removed along the center line of the fillet. Lightly salt the fish. Fold over the ends of the cheesecloth to enclose the fish.

2. Prepare the poaching broth: In a fish poacher or shallow pot large enough to hold the fish in a single piece, combine the kelp and cold water and bring the water to a boil. Remove from the heat, and season with the rice wine.

3. Carefully place the wrapped fish in the poaching broth, skin side down. Arrange the kelp so that it rests on top of the fish, almost like an inner lid. Over low heat, poach the fish for 8–10 minutes. Ladle the poaching liquid over the kelp and fish frequently.

4. Remove the pot from the heat, and allow the fish to cool in the poaching broth. Then remove the fish from the broth and chill it, still wrapped in cheesecloth and covered with kelp, in the refrigerator for at least 1 hour and up to 12 hours.

5. Prepare the fiddleheads: Trim the dark, discolored stems from the fiddleheads. Dissolve the alum in enough cold water to cover the fiddleheads, then soak the trimmed fronds in the alum solution for at least 10 minutes and up to 1 hour. (This will keep them bright green and remove the slight bitterness that many fiddleheads have.) Rinse the fiddleheads under fresh cold water.

6. Bring a pot of fresh water to a rolling boil. Blanch the fiddleheads for 5–6 minutes, or until just tender. Drain, and let them cool to room temperature, then chill if you wish.

7. Make the mustard sauce: In a small saucepan combine the bean paste, sugar, soy sauce, and vinegar. Stir well with a wooden spoon or paddle until smooth. Place the mixture over medium heat and cook the sauce, stirring, until bubbly and

glossy and slightly thickened. Remove the pan from the heat and let the mixture cool slightly; then stir in the mustard. Cover, and chill the sauce for at least 1 hour, or up to 1 week, in the refrigerator. Just before using, thin the sauce to the consistency of heavy cream with the stock or water.

8. Slice the poached fish into three or four pieces and serve, skin side down, with the sauce poured over the white flesh and a small mound of fiddleheads to the side.

TO BE DEEP-FRIED

Fried Soft-Shelled Crabs in a Spicy Sauce
Kani Kara Agé no Momiji Oroshi

Serves 2

Although all species of crabs molt and, theoretically at least, could be a soft-shelled delicacy, the commercial catch in the United States comes primarily from the Chesapeake Bay area. There, tasty tiny blue crabs are harvested before their shells harden and are brought to market. Soft-shelled crabs are not part of traditional Japanese cuisine, but here in the United States in the early summer, nearly every Japanese restaurant serves them deep-fried, crispy, and crunchy!

> *4 small soft-shelled crabs*

MARINADE:

> *¼ cup* saké *(Japanese rice wine)*
> *1½ tablespoons soy sauce*

DIPPING SAUCE:

⅓ *cup* dashi (*basic sea stock, page 27*)

1 *tablespoon* mirin (*syrupy rice wine*)

1 *tablespoon soy sauce*

1 *tablespoon fresh lemon juice*

1 *packet* (*3–5 grams*) katsuo bushi (*dried bonito flakes*)

3 *tablespoons cornstarch*

oil for deep-frying

CONDIMENTS:

3 *tablespoons grated* daikon (*Japanese white radish*)

¼ *teaspoon powdered* ichimi tōgarashi (*chili pepper*)

2 *tablespoons finely chopped scallions* (*green part only*) OR *chives*

1. Have your fish store clean the crabs for you. Cut each crab in half, between the eyes and through the center of the body, with a sharp knife. Combine the rice wine and soy sauce, and marinate the crabs in the mixture while you make the sauce.

2. Combine the sea stock, syrupy rice wine, soy sauce, and lemon juice in a small saucepan. Simmer the sauce for 1 minute, then remove the pan from the heat and sprinkle in the fish flakes. Let the sauce sit for 2 minutes, then stir, and strain through a cloth- or paper-lined colander. Keep the sauce warm.

3. Remove the crabs from the marinade and pat them with paper towels to absorb the excess moisture; they will still be moist. Dust the crabs with the cornstarch and allow them to sit for 5 minutes, or until the cornstarch becomes slightly reddish brown in color.

4. Heat the oil in a deep-fryer or wok to about 370 degrees. Test with a pinch of cornstarch moistened with soy sauce: The cornstarch will sink ever so slightly, then rise immediately to sizzle on the surface but not color rapidly. Fry the crab pieces, two at a time, for 1½ minutes or until crisp and nicely colored. Drain the fried crabs on paper towels.

5. To serve, reassemble the crabs (four half-pieces for each portion) on plates lined with doilies or other decorative paper liners. Divide the dipping sauce between two shallow bowls or deeply rimmed plates.

6. With your fingers, gently press the grated radish to the side of the bowl in which it sits and pour off excess accumulated liquid. Stir in the powdered chili pepper. Coax this red-flecked radish mixture into two mounds. Divide the scallions into two portions, and use one to crown each of the radish mountains. Place these condiments on the plate next to the crabs. To eat, each person adds condiments to his or her liking to the dipping sauce before dunking the fried crabs in it.

Crunchy Fried Shrimp
Ebi Furai

This is unquestionably one of the most popular dishes in Japan. Its fans range from the nursery-school set—for whom these breaded fried shrimp are a favorite lunch-box treat—to full-fledged grown-ups, who never seem to tire of eating the crunchy crustaceans at home and in restaurants.

Serves 4 as a main course, 6–8 as an appetizer

2 dozen large shrimp, with shells and tails intact
¼ cup all-purpose flour
¼ teaspoon salt
1 large egg
2 tablespoons cold water
1½ cups panko (*Japanese coarse bread crumbs*)
   corn, soy, OR other vegetable oil for deep-frying
   few drops goma abura (*aromatic sesame oil*), *optional*
   tonkatsu sōsu (*a thick, dark, spicy sauce*), *optional*

1. Remove the shells from the shrimp, keeping the last segment and tail intact. Make a shallow slit down the curved back of each shrimp and remove the vein. Flip the shrimp over and make two or three shallow diagonal slits across the underbelly. Gently press on these slits to straighten out the shrimp and keep them from curling further when fried. Rinse the shrimp quickly under cold water, then pat them dry.

2. Season the flour with the salt, and lightly dredge each shrimp in the mixture, being sure to dredge the tails well. Beat the egg and cold water together, and dip an entire shrimp in the mixture, then toss it into the coarse bread crumbs. Shake the bowl of crumbs a bit to coat each shrimp thoroughly. Repeat with all the shrimp. You can bread the shrimp

These shrimp are wonderfully crunchy because they're coated with small, coarse, pointy shards of bread called panko. *Try using Japanese* panko *the next time you want extra-crunchy fried fish, chicken, or veal or pork cutlets.*

 149

several hours before frying them, if you need to. Transfer them to a paper-lined plate and refrigerate, but bring them back to room temperature before frying.

3. Pour at least 2 inches of oil into a wok or other deep-fryer. If you add a few drops of aromatic sesame oil, it will impart a marvelous nutty taste. Heat the oil to approximately 350 degrees. Test the temperature with a few bread crumbs that have egg wash on them. They should gently sizzle on the surface, coloring slowly to a golden hue.

4. Fry the shrimp in two or three batches for about 1½ minutes. The breading will turn golden, and the meat opaque and firm. Flip the shrimp once during the frying, about halfway through. Drain well on paper towels.

5. Serve with the thick, dark, spicy sauce drizzled over them. The shrimp are delicious hot or at room temperature.

Crisp-and-Fiery Catfish Fry

Namazu no Kara Agé

In America, catfish used to be a local southern dish, enjoyed by ordinary folks. In recent years, thanks to the popularity of Cajun and Creole cooking, the once-lowly catfish has become an American delicacy. Japanese restaurants in the United States most often serve it deep-fried, with just a dusting of cornstarch and a fiery dipping sauce.

Serves 2

6–8 *ounces fillet of catfish, skinned*
   1 *tablespoon soy sauce*

DIPPING SAUCE:
   ¼ *cup* dashi (*basic sea stock, page 27*)
   1 *tablespoon* mirin (*syrupy rice wine*)
   1 *tablespoon* usukuchi shōyu (*light soy sauce*)
   pinch ichimi tōgarashi (*powdered red chili pepper*)

GARNISH:
   1 *small lemon* OR *lime*

2–3 *tablespoons cornstarch*
   vegetable oil for deep-frying

1. With a sharp knife held at a 45-degree angle to the cutting board, slice the fish slightly on the diagonal, to make 8–10 pieces. Each piece should be about 1½ to 2 inches square and fairly even in thickness.

2. Toss the fish in the soy sauce, then let it marinate for 5–10 minutes while you make the dipping sauce.

3. In a small saucepan, combine the sea stock, syrupy rice wine, and light soy sauce, and simmer for about 3 minutes to allow the flavors to meld. Stir in the powdered chili pepper, and set the sauce aside.

4. Cut the lemon or lime in half lengthwise. Cut each half lengthwise into five wedges. Arrange the wedges to resemble a feather, and garnish each plate with a lemon or lime "feather."

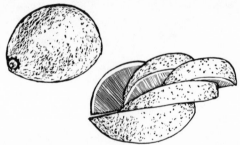

5. Remove the fish from the soy sauce and pat off excess soy with paper towels. Dust the fish with the cornstarch, and set it aside for 5 minutes. The coating will turn reddish brown as it absorbs the soy.

6. Fill a wok or other deep-fryer with 1½–2 inches of oil. Heat the oil to about 375 degrees. Test the temperature with a pinch of cornstarch moistened with soy sauce. It should sizzle and slowly turn to a light gold.

7. At the table, each person adds a squeeze of lemon or lime juice to the dipping sauce. To eat, dip the fried fish in the seasoned sauce.

Curry-Flavored Fried Fish

Agé-Zakana, Indo Fū

Not all foreign influence upon the Japanese diet has been Western. China and India have lent many spices and cooking techniques over the past centuries as well. The Japanese have a particular fondness for curry flavoring, using it both to season stews served over rice and in batter-fried fish. Here, the bright golden fried fish combines the flavors of India and Japan.

Serves 4

12–14 ounces fillet of sole or flounder

1–2 teaspoons all-purpose flour

CURRY BATTER:

1 egg

ice water

2–3 teaspoons curry powder

scant ⅔ cup self-rising cake flour

vegetable oil for deep-frying

1 small lime, cut into four wedges

1. Lay the fillet of fish on a cutting board, and with a sharp knife held at a 45-degree angle to the board, slice the fish slightly on the diagonal into twelve pieces of equal size and thickness. In Japanese, this cutting technique is called *sogi-giri.*

2. Lay the slices of fish so that the surface of each piece is fully exposed on the board, then sift a light dusting of all-purpose flour over one side, then the other.

3. In a bowl, combine the egg and enough ice water to make ⅔ cup. Stir the curry powder into the self-rising flour, then sift this mixture over the egg-water. Stir to barely moisten; the batter should be lumpy.

4. Fill a wok or other deep-fryer with 1½–2 inches of oil. Heat the oil to about 360 degrees. Test the temperature with a few drops of the batter: It should sink, then rise right away, puffing up on the surface of the oil with bubbles surrounding it. Dip the fish, one piece at a time, into the curry batter and then gently lower it into the oil. Fry two or three pieces of fish at one time. Turn the fish once or twice during the cooking time; 2–2½ minutes should be sufficient to cook the fish through and make the golden batter crisp. Drain the fish on paper towels.

5. Repeat to fry all the fish. If you like, preheat your oven to 250 degrees and keep the first few batches warm in the oven while you continue to fry. Serve the fish hot, three pieces per person, with lime wedges on the side.

Mackerel Fried in Sesame Batter, Southern Japanese Style

Aji no Nambu Agé

Japanese waters yield an abundant supply of *aji*, or horse mackerel, and it appears regularly on home and restaurant tables. American waters have a generous supply of mackerel, too, though of a slightly different variety than the petite Japanese *aji*. For this recipe, both varieties work equally well.

This particular preparation—dipped in a sesame-sprinkled batter and deep-fried—is what the Japanese refer to as "southern fried," or *nambu agé*. Quite different from what we associate with below our Mason-Dixon Line, this fried fish dish is nonetheless mighty tasty.

Serves 4

> *3 large mackerel fillets, about 12–14 ounces in all*
>
> *1 tablespoon* saké *(Japanese rice wine)*
>
> *¼ teaspoon salt*

BATTER:

> *½ cup all-purpose flour*
>
> *½ teaspoon baking soda*
>
> *1 egg yolk*
>
> *cold water*
>
> *1½ tablespoons black sesame seeds*
>
> *vegetable oil for deep-frying*

1. Cut the fillets slightly on the diagonal, to help even out the thickness of each piece. Cut the fish into twelve pieces in all. Toss the pieces with the rice wine, sprinkle them with the salt, and set aside while making the batter.

2. In a bowl, sift together the flour and baking soda. In a measuring cup, mix the egg yolk with enough cold water to make ¼–⅓ cup. The greater quantity of water will produce a slightly more delicate coating. Add the flour mixture to the egg mixture, and stir to combine.

3. In a clean, dry skillet, toast the sesame seeds for 30–40 seconds over high heat. Keep the skillet in motion to ensure even heat. Add the sesame seeds to the batter, and stir to mix in.

4. You will need at least 1½–2 inches of oil in a deep-fryer or wok to fry the fish properly. Heat the oil to about 365 degrees. Test the oil with a few drops of batter: it should sink ever so slightly, then rise and puff immediately on the surface. The batter should continue to bubble and sizzle on the surface, coloring very slightly after 1 minute or so.

5. Dip the fish fillets in the batter, and then fry them, in batches, for about 3 minutes each, turning once or twice during frying. The coating should be crisp and golden, the fish tender and moist. Drain the fish on paper towels and serve immediately for the best texture. If necessary, the fried fish can be held, uncovered and on a rack, in a 200-degree oven for up to 30 minutes.

Crispy Japanese-Style Tuna Croquettes

Tsuna Korokké

Serves 2–3

Although deep-frying came to Japanese cuisine relatively late in its history (the Portuguese are credited with giving the idea of batter-fried fish—*tempura*—to the Japanese in the seventeenth century), it is still a very popular cooking method. In addition to lacy batter-fried foods, the Japanese also favor a crisp and crunchy breading made from coarse, pointy shards of bread. Such breaded fried foods remain crisp even at room temperature, and croquettes like these are often packed into lunch boxes. At home, these *korokké* might be served in the evening with a bowl of hot *miso* soup, steaming rice, and pickled vegetables.

> *1 can (6½ ounces) tuna fish*
>
> *1 tablespoon fresh lemon juice*

BINDER:

> *½ tablespoon butter*
>
> *¼ cup all-purpose flour*
>
> *½ cup milk, scalded*
>
> *pinch salt*
>
> *pinch* sansho (*fragrant Japanese pepper*)

> *¼ cup fresh* OR *frozen tiny peas, defrosted if frozen*
>
> *½ sheet* yaki nori (*paper-thin toasted seaweed*), *optional*
>
> *1–2 tablespoons flour, for dusting*
>
> *1 egg beaten with 1 tablespoon cold water*
>
> *½–⅔ cup* panko (*Japanese coarse bread crumbs*)
>
> *oil for deep-frying*
>
> *lemon wedges*

 **157**

1. Drain the tuna of its packing water or oil. Mix the tuna with the lemon juice, flaking the tuna as you do this.

2. Make the binder in a small saucepan: Melt the butter, then sprinkle the flour over it. Cook this roux for 2 minutes over low heat. Add the hot milk and whisk to make a smooth white sauce. Cook for 1 minute to thicken the sauce. Season with the salt and fragrant pepper. Remove the saucepan from the heat.

3. Stir the flaked tuna into the white sauce.

4. Blanch fresh peas in boiling salted water to cover for 2 minutes, or until barely tender, then drain. If you are using frozen peas, merely defrost and drain them. Add the peas to the white sauce and tuna mixture. Cover, and chill this mixture for at least 30 minutes and up to 24 hours.

5. Form the chilled tuna mixture into eight or nine ovals (eight if you want to serve two people four croquettes each, nine if you want to serve three people three croquettes each).

6. If you want to add extra nutrition and color contrast, cut the paper-thin seaweed into eight or nine strips and wrap a band of seaweed around the center of each croquette. Dust the croquettes with the flour, dip them into the egg wash, and then roll them in the bread crumbs.

7. Fill a wok or other deep-fryer with 1½–2 inches of oil. Heat the oil to about 375 degrees. Test with a few bread crumbs, preferably ones to which a bit of the egg wash is clinging: The crumbs should sink ever so slightly, rise, and sizzle on the surface, coloring slowly. Deep-fry the croquettes, two or three at a time, for 2½–3 minutes, until golden and heated through. Drain the croquettes on paper towels, and serve hot or at room temperature, with lemon wedges on the side.

Mixed Fry of Shrimp and Smelts
Tempura

The Japanese excel in making light, lacy fries of fish and seafood. One secret is in mixing the batter: Use only icy cold water (to retard the sticky action of the gluten in the flour), and combine batter and ingredients at the last moment, just before frying. Another secret is in maintaining the right temperature of the oil: It should be hot enough to make the batter puff and sizzle immediately, but not so hot that the batter browns right away.

Serves 4

8 *large shrimp, with shells and tails intact*

12 *whole small smelts* OR *10 ounces fillet of sole*

BATTER:

1 *egg*

ice water

⅔ *cup self-rising cake flour*

vegetable oil for deep-frying

DIPPING SAUCE:

1 *cup* dashi (*basic sea stock, page 27*) OR *water*

¼ *cup soy sauce*

¼ *cup* mirin (*syrupy rice wine*)

1 *packet (5 grams)* katsuo bushi (*dried bonito flakes*)

CONDIMENTS:

3–4 *tablespoons grated* daikon (*white Japanese radish*)

2 *teaspoons grated fresh ginger*

1. Remove the shell from the shrimp, keeping the tail and last segment intact. With a knife, make a shallow slit down the back of each shrimp and devein it. Turn each shrimp over and make two or three shallow diagonal slits across the belly. Press gently against these slits to just break the tight muscles but not so much that the shrimp falls apart. This will help to keep the shrimp from curling when frying.

2. Wash the smelts, and scrape off the scales. Remove the head of each smelt, then slit the belly to the tail and remove the internal organs. Press gently with your fingers to butterfly the fish. If you bend the fish back, you can easily peel away the skeletal structure. Cut off the bones at the tail.

   If you are using fillet of sole, slice the fish, slightly on the diagonal, into twelve pieces, each about 1 x 2 inches and ⅛ inch thick.

3. In a bowl, mix the egg and enough ice water to make ⅔ cup. Set aside 1 tablespoon flour from the measured ingredients, and sift the remaining flour over the liquid. With chopsticks or a fork, barely mix the flour and egg-water. There should be plenty of lumps, and flour should still be sticking to the sides of the bowl. Dust the shrimp and smelts or sole with the reserved tablespoon of flour.

4. Fill a wok or other deep-fryer with 1½–2 inches of oil. Heat the oil to about 370 degrees. Test with a bit of batter: It should sink ever so slightly, rise and puff on the surface immediately, and sizzle but not brown quickly.

5. Dip the shrimp in the batter, shaking excess batter back into the bowl. Carefully lay the shrimp in the oil. Dip another shrimp and repeat the procedure. Flip the shrimp once, then let them fry, undisturbed, for 1 minute. Flip again and let them fry for 30–40 seconds. The meat will become opaque and the batter crisp and golden. Drain on paper towel-lined racks.

Don't discard the fish flakes after making the sauce. Save them to make Ocean Confetti (on page 217).

 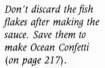

6. Repeat the dipping and frying to cook the remaining shrimp and the smelts or sole. You can keep the cooked *tempura* warm in a preheated 300-degree oven.

7. In a small saucepan, combine the sea stock or water, soy sauce, and syrupy rice wine. Stir and simmer for 2–3 minutes, then remove from the heat. Sprinkle the fish flakes over the sauce, and let them steep for 3 minutes. Strain the sauce and divide it among four attractive bowls that can be used for dipping.

8. Arrange two fried shrimp and three fried smelts or pieces of sole on each of four plates. Divide the grated radish into four portions and coax each portion into a mountain shape. Top each radish mountain with a portion of the grated ginger. Place one of these two-toned mountains on the side of each plate of *tempura*.

Lacy Seafood Pancakes
Kaki Agé

Serves 2

A variation on the theme of batter-fried foods, these lacy pancakes are typically made of bits and pieces of leftovers. Freshly fried and piping hot, the crispy pancakes need only a squeeze of lemon and/or a pinch of salt and fragrant pepper to bring out their fine flavor. And any leftover pancakes are delicious the next day, when you can serve them over rice with a robust soy-flavored sauce (see the next recipe, *Tendon*).

SHRIMP FILLING:

> 4 *small shrimp, peeled, deveined, and chopped into ¼-inch pieces*
>
> 1 *slender scallion, trimmed and chopped*
>
> 1 *slender zucchini, about 3 ounces, trimmed and sliced on the diagonal, then across into ¼-inch julienne strips*

SQUID FILLING:

> ¼–⅓ *cup chopped squid (the legs and "wings" left over from the Squid and Endive Salad on page 126)*
>
> 2 *slender scallions, trimmed and chopped*
>
> 1 *baking potato, about 3 ounces, peeled and cut into ½-inch julienne strips*

BATTER:

> 1 *egg*
>
> *ice water*
>
> ⅔ *cup self-rising cake flour*
>
> *vegetable oil for deep-frying*

CONDIMENTS:

> *lemon wedges*
>
> ¼ *teaspoon salt*
>
> ⅛ *teaspoon* sansho (*fragrant Japanese pepper*)

1. Combine the shrimp filling ingredients in one small bowl, the squid filling ingredients in another.

2. Beat the egg with enough ice water to make ⅔ cup, and pour into bowl. Sift the flour over the liquid, and with chopsticks or a fork, barely mix the two. There should be plenty of lumps, and flour should still be sticking to the sides of the bowl.

3. Fill a wok or other deep-fryer with 1½–2 inches of oil. Heat the oil to about 370 degrees. Test the temperature with a few drops of batter: It should sink ever so slightly, rise and puff on the surface immediately, and sizzle but not brown quickly.

4. Pour half the batter over the shrimp filling ingredients. Use a small-mesh strainer to scoop up about one quarter of the filling ingredients. Allow excess batter to drip through the mesh back into the bowl. Gently pour the batter-bound ingredients into the hot oil to make a 3-inch pancake. If many bits disperse, lower the heat ever so slightly, and use chopsticks to retrieve the wayward pieces and place them on top of the still-uncooked batter in the center of the pancake. If there seems to be too little batter binding the ingredients, add a bit where you think necessary. It is usually best to err on the stingy side.

5. Flip the pancake and then let it fry, undisturbed, for 1–1½ minutes. Flip the pancake back again and fry for another 30 seconds. Remove the pancake to a paper-towel-lined rack and proceed to make three more shrimp-filled pancakes in the same manner. If you are trying this recipe for the first time, it's best to make one pancake at a time; once you get the knack of it, you can fry two or three at a time in a 12- to 16-inch-wide wok or other deep frying pan. You can keep the shrimp pancakes warm in a preheated 300-degree oven.

6. Add the remaining batter to the squid pancake ingredients and proceed to make four pancakes in the same manner as

The key to success in making these lacy pancakes is to use as little batter as possible, just enough to hold the ingredients together.

 163

you did the shrimp. It's important to combine the batter and ingredients at the last moment, just before you are ready to fry them.

7. Serve the pancakes hot, two of each kind to each person. Mix the salt and pepper together, and serve the lemon wedges and salt-and-pepper mixture on the side. Each person squeezes lemon juice and sprinkles the salt-and-pepper mixture over his or her own pancakes while eating.

Leftover Seafood Pancakes on Rice
Tendon

Serves 4

Although *tempura* is probably tastiest when freshly made and piping hot, serving it over rice with a sauce certainly makes terrific-tasting leftovers! Use either the Mixed Fry of Shrimp and Smelts on page 159 or the Lacy Seafood Pancakes on page 162 to make this filling meal-in-a-bowl.

4–8 pieces leftover tempura (*page 159*) *and/or* kaki agé (*page 162*)

4 cups cooked rice (page 213)

SAUCE:

½ cup dashi (*basic sea stock, page 27*) OR *water*

2 tablespoons soy sauce

2 tablespoons mirin (*syrupy rice wine*)

1 packet (5 grams) katsuo bushi (*dried bonito flakes*)

1. Heat the already cooked *tempura* or *kaki agé* pancakes in a low (300-degree) oven for 5 minutes.

2. If the rice is not piping hot, reheat it in a microwave oven: It's simplest to use microwave-safe individual deep bowls for serving the final dish. Fill each of the four bowls with a cup of rice. Cover each bowl with clear plastic wrap, and use a toothpick to poke several holes in the wrap to vent steam. Cook the rice on medium (about 490 watts) for 1½ minutes.

If you don't have a microwave, reheat your rice in the top of a covered double boiler.

3. In a small saucepan, combine the stock or water and the soy sauce and syrupy rice wine. Stir and simmer for 2–3 minutes, then remove the pan from the heat. Sprinkle the fish flakes over the sauce, and let them steep for 3 minutes. Strain the sauce.

4. To serve, place one or two pieces of warm *tempura* or *kaki agé* pancakes on top of each bowl of hot rice. Pour a few tablespoons of sauce over each portion.

Don't discard the fish flakes after making the sauce. Save them to make Ocean Confetti, page 217.

Steam-Baked Trout Stuffed with *Miso*

Nijimasu no Dengaku Tsutsumi

Serves 4

This recipe is for sport fishermen—or anyone lucky enough to receive the bounty of their catch. The Japanese prototype is made by skewering whole tiny *ayu* trout, smearing them with bean paste, and setting them to cook at an open hearth. The recipe I give here, with the fish wrapped in foil, will work over an outdoor campfire or grill and indoors too, in an oven. Rainbow trout are the tastiest fish, I think, prepared this way, although shad is also marvelous when stuffed with the pungent bean sauce.

4 whole trout, about 4–6 ounces each

NERI MISO SAUCE:

  ¼ cup Sendai miso OR *other dark fermented bean paste*

  3 tablespoons sugar

  2 tablespoons saké (*Japanese rice wine*)

  1 slender scallion OR *small bunch fresh chives*

A mixture of miso, *sugar, and rice wine—called* neri miso—*is used to season and sauce all manner of fish, poultry, and vegetable dishes in the classic Japanese kitchen. Double or triple the quantities given here and store extra* neri miso *sauce in a glass jar in your refrigerator. It will keep for up to 2 weeks and then you'll have it on hand to make sea scallops with* miso (*page 102*) *and Bluefish Poached in* Miso (*page 200*).

1. Rinse the fishes well, then with the back of your knife, scrape the fine, sticky scales off the skin. Make a slit from just

166

below the gills down the belly line, remove the viscera, and rinse the fishes well, then pat them dry. Lay each fish on a 10-inch square of aluminum foil with its shiny side facing up.

2. Combine the sauce ingredients in a small saucepan, and stir to mix them well. Place the saucepan over medium heat and cook, stirring, until the sauce is bubbly and glossy. Simmer for another minute, stirring constantly.

3. Stuff the trouts' belly cavities with the pungent bean sauce, then spread any leftover sauce over the top of each fish. Fold the foil to enclose each trout in a sealed pocket.

4. Place the packets on a rack suspended over a hot grill, only an inch or two from the coals, or on the top rack in a hot oven (400 degrees). Bake the fish for 10–12 minutes.

5. Trim the scallion, then slice it into thin julienne strips on the diagonal. Rinse these strips briefly in cold water, drain, and squeeze dry. Or, mince the chives. After each person opens a packet of aromatic fish, he or she garnishes it with some scallions or chives.

Steamed Flounder Stuffed with Noodles

Hiramé no Soba Mushi

Serves 2

This entrée is low in calories, high in nutrition, and packed with flavor and texture surprises. The Japanese most often serve this dish with assorted pickled vegetables and a *miso*-thickened soup. A large tossed green salad completes this meal just as nicely.

1 fillet of flounder, about 7–8 ounces

MARINADE:

1 tablespoon saké (*Japanese rice wine*)
¼ teaspoon salt

1 ounce dried soba (*buckwheat noodles*)
⅓ cup Tosa dashi (*smoky sea stock, page 28*)

CONDIMENTS:

1 tablespoon grated daikon (*Japanese white radish*), *drained*
1 tablespoon finely chopped scallion, green part only
½ tablespoon grated fresh ginger

1. Slice the fillet in half lengthwise. Combine the rice wine and salt in a flat dish, and marinate the fish in the mixture while cooking the noodles.

2. Bring a large pot of water to a rolling boil. Add the buckwheat noodles and cook for 5 minutes once the water has returned to a boil. The noodles will still be firm. Drain, and rinse the noodles under cold water to remove excess starch and to stop the cooking. Drain again.

3. Remove one of the pieces of fish fillet from the marinade and lay it, smooth side down, on a cutting board. Lay half the noodles across the center of the fish. Roll the fish over the noodles to enclose them. Place this packet, seam side down, in a steamproof or microwave-safe shallow bowl or deeply rimmed dish. (Broad, shallow soup bowls are often a good choice.) Repeat the rolling process with the remaining fillet of fish and noodles; place this packet on a separate dish.

4. You can either steam the fish or use a microwave oven to cook this dish; the latter is faster and yields prettier results without compromising on flavor.

For the microwave: Cover the dishes snugly with clear plastic wrap, then poke several holes in the wrap to vent steam as the fish cooks. Cook the noodle-stuffed fish for 2 minutes on high setting (100 percent power or 600 watts). Remove the dishes from the oven and pour off any liquid that may have accumulated. Divide the Smoky Sea Stock between the two dishes and pour it over the noodle-stuffed fish. Cover the dishes again, poke several holes to vent steam, and cook for another 40 seconds on high.

To steam: Bring the water in the bottom of a large steamer to a rolling boil over high heat. Lower the heat to allow for a steady flow of steam and cook the fish, covered, for 3 minutes. Carefully remove the lid from your steamer, and use paper towels to blot up any excess liquid that has accumulated in the bowls or dishes. Divide the Smoky Sea Stock between the two portions, and pour it over the fish. Cover the steamer again and cook for 2 minutes. Remove the steamer from the heat, and let the fish "settle" for another 2–3 minutes. Use pot holders to carefully remove the very hot dishes from the steamer.

5. Place a mound of grated radish, a mound of grated ginger, and a mound of chopped green scallions on top of each portion of fish. Serve immediately. Each diner takes these condiments and swishes them in the pool of sauce surrounding the fish.

If you plan to use a steamer to make this dish, use one that has a flat surface on which to rest your plates; the popular adjustable aluminum baskets that fit into many pots won't work here. You can improvise a flat-surfaced steamer: Remove top and bottom from two cans of the same height. Stand these in a deep pot. Fill the pot with water to just below the top rim of the cans. Rest your plate or plates on the cans.

To facilitate removal of the hot plates later, fashion a sling from a length of cheesecloth or other fabric. The sling should be under your plate before you rest it on either a flat-surfaced rack or the cans of your improvised steamer. Place the lid on your pot or steamer, then tie up the ends of the sling over the cover, for safety.

 **169**

Steamed Shad Infused with Ginger and Scallions

Nishin no Shōga Mushi

Serves 4

Shad heralds spring along the eastern seaboard of the United States, and both the flesh and roe are prized. Here I've borrowed a robust gingery preparation from the Japanese to enhance the natural sweetness of this native American fish. Another, and very different, way of preparing shad can be found in the recipe for *miso*-stuffed trout on page 166.

2 large fillets of shad, about 14 ounces in all, boned

MARINADE:

2 tablespoons saké *(Japanese rice wine)*
½ teaspoon ginger juice (extracted from grated fresh ginger)

4 slender scallions

1. Rinse the fish under cold water and gently pat it dry with paper towels. Cut each fillet in half, crosswise, yielding four servings of about 3–4 ounces each.

2. Combine the rice wine and ginger juice in a glass loaf pan. Marinate the fish for 5 minutes, turning the pieces occasionally to ensure even flavoring.

3. Trim the scallions, then cut them into julienne strips on the diagonal. Lift the flap of flesh created by boning the shad fillet, and sprinkle the white and green scallion strips between the meat and the skin.

4. Place each portion of fish on a piece of aluminum foil with its shiny side up, measuring about 5 x 8 inches. Fold the foil over the fish, sealing the sides by folding or crimping.

5. Bring the water in a steamer to a boil, then adjust the heat to maintain a steady flow of steam. Place the packets in the steamer and cook the fish for 5 minutes. Serve a single packet to each person, hot.

Sea-Steamed Snapper

Chiri Mushi

Kelp adds a subtlety to foods and liquids cooked with it. No wonder the Japanese use it often to prepare delicate steamed dishes. Here the kelp imparts that incomparable saltwater aroma and brings out the natural sweet flavor of the snapper. Tilefish is also very tasty prepared this way.

Serves 4

4 *2-inch lengths* dashi kombu (*dried kelp for stock making*)

1½ *cups cold water*

3–4 *fresh* shiitaké (*dark oak*) *mushrooms, about 1 ounce*

1 *tablespoon soy sauce, preferably* usukuchi shōyu (*light soy sauce*)

2 *teaspoons* mirin (*syrupy rice wine*)

4 *small filets of snapper, about 14–16 ounces in all*

1 *tablespoon* saké (*Japanese rice wine*)

¼ *teaspoon salt*

2 *teaspoons cornstarch*

1 *teaspoon cold water*

1½ *teaspoons grated fresh ginger*

1. Place the kelp in a saucepan with the cold water, and bring it to a boil over high heat. Remove the kelp, and set the pieces aside.

 **171**

2. Remove the stems from the mushrooms and add them to the kelp broth. (Set aside the mushroom caps.) Continue to cook the broth over medium heat for 10–15 minutes, or until it has been reduced by half. Strain the broth through a cloth- or paper-lined strainer, and season it with the soy sauce and syrupy rice wine.

3. Toss the fish in the rice wine, then sprinkle the fillets with the salt.

4. In each of four heatproof, deeply rimmed plates (or wide, shallow bowls), lay a piece of softened kelp. Lay a fish fillet on top of each piece of kelp, skin side down.

5. Brush the mushroom caps to remove any gritty material that may be clinging to them. Cut the caps into julienne slices, and scatter them across the four portions of fish.

6. Bring the water in the bottom of a steamer to a boil (for a discussion of steamers, see page 169). Adjust the heat to maintain a steady flow of steam. Cover, and steam the fish for 3–4 minutes, or until the fish looks barely opaque.

7. Combine the cornstarch and cold water to form a thick paste. Bring the kelp and mushroom broth to a rolling boil. Add the cornstarch paste, stirring constantly to thicken the sauce. Spoon enough sauce over each portion of fish and mushrooms to moisten them well; reserve the remaining

sauce for later. Continue to steam, covered, for 4–5 more minutes, the longer time for fish more than 1 inch thick.

8. Carefully remove the plates from the steamer, and just before serving, pour the remaining thickened sauce over the fish and garnish each portion with a small mound of grated ginger. Each person can then dissolve as much of the condiment as they wish in the warm sauce surrounding their portion of fish. Serve immediately.

Steam-Baked Ocean Perch with Lemon and Snow Peas
Akadai no Gingami Mushi

The bright scarlet skin and sweet, firm, snowy flesh of ocean perch make it a prized fish in Japan, where the colors red and white mean happiness. This dish is sure to make calorie-counting Americans happy: less than 150 calories for this meaty entrée garnished with crisp, bright green snow peas.

Serves 2

> *2 fillets ocean perch or redfish, 3–4 ounces each, scales removed but with skin intact*
> *½ tablespoon saké (Japanese rice wine)*
> *pinch salt*
> *10 thin slices lemon*
> *6 fresh snow peas*

1. Rinse the fillets under cold running water, and pat the fish dry. Remove any belly bones with tweezers. Sprinkle the flesh of the fish with the rice wine, then lightly salt the flesh.

173

2. Across the center of each of two 10 x 12-inch pieces of aluminum foil, arrange two slices of lemon, side by side. Lay a fillet of fish, with its bright red skin facing up, over each row of lemon slices. Arrange three more circles of lemon over each piece of fish, slightly overlapping the slices.

3. Snap back the stem end of each snow pea and remove the string, if any. Stack the snow peas and slice them on the diagonal into julienne strips. Scatter these across the lemon slices on each piece of fish.

4. Bring the edges of the foil together and seal each packet. Bring the water in the bottom of a steamer to a boil. Adjust the heat to maintain a steady flow of steam. Place the packets in the steamer, and cook 7–8 minutes. Serve the packets sealed, so that each person gets to enjoy the aroma as he or she opens the packet up at the table.

TO BE BROILED, GRILLED, OR SKILLET-GLAZED

Miso-Marinated Broiled Flounder

Hiramé no Miso-Zuké Yaki

Serves 4–6

In the days before refrigeration, fresh fish fillets were often kept from spoiling by placing them in a paste made of fermented soybeans. The mildly tangy taste that resulted from this ancient method is obviously appealing to modern Japanese, too, since they continue to crave *miso-zuké,* or "fermented bean paste–marinated" fish. You'll come to love *miso*-marinated fish, too, for its convenience (pick up several extra fillets at the fish market and enjoy them days later) and its fine flavor.

12–14 ounces fillet of flounder

REUSABLE MARINADE:

    2–3 cups shiro miso (*light fermented bean paste*)

    2–3 tablespoons mirin (*syrupy rice wine*)

    2–3 tablespoons saké (*Japanese rice wine*)

1. Cut the flounder into four to six portions. Slicing it on the diagonal will help to even out the thickness of the pieces.

2. Blend the marinade ingredients, and use half the mixture to line the bottom of a glass or ceramic pan just large enough to hold the fish in a single layer. Lay a double or triple layer of cheesecloth over the marinade. Lay the fish over the cloth, and then cover the fish with more cheesecloth. Spread the remaining marinade on top, to completely cover the cloth. Cover the entire arrangement with clear plastic wrap and refrigerate for 3 to 36 hours. (Or leave at room temperature for up to 2 hours before cooking.)

The fermented bean paste marinade can be reused many times. Pour off any accumulated liquid. Scrape the marinade from the cloth, and store the seasoned miso paste in a glass jar in the refrigerator. It can be reused up to three or four times within a period of 4–6 weeks. Fresh cheesecloth should be used each time.

If you grill outdoors, this marinated fish is delicious cooked over mildly aromatic wood such as mesquite. To prevent undue charring, grill rather slowly over low or dying embers.

3. Preheat the broiler to medium-high. Remove the fish from the marinade, and place the fillets on a rack (disposable foil broiling pans are fine) 2–3 inches from the source of heat. Broil the fish for 3 minutes, then flip the fillets and broil for 2–3 more minutes. Check the progress and adjust the heat accordingly. The cooked fish will be golden brown, with a slightly crusty surface and succulent, firm flesh within. Probably a total of 7–8 minutes is necessary to achieve this.

Salt-Grilled Kingfish

Sawara no Shio Yaki

Serves 4

Salt-grilling is probably the single most common cooking technique the Japanese use for fish. An ancient method, it still has obvious appeal, since the fish remains moist within and slightly crusty outside. If you wish to limit your sodium intake, leave the skin behind.

4 kingfish steaks, about 4–5 ounces each
2 tablespoons saké (*Japanese rice wine*)
½ teaspoon salt, preferably coarse
½ lemon
½ cup grated daikon (*Japanese white radish*), *optional*
　soy sauce, optional

1. Rinse each of the fish steaks under fresh cold water, then pat them dry. Let the fish marinate in the rice wine for 5–10 minutes, turning the fish once halfway through.

2. Preheat your broiler to the highest setting possible, or if you are grilling outdoors, make sure your coals are burning hot.

3. Remove the fish from the marinade, and very lightly salt the flesh on both sides. Salt the surrounding skin a bit more generously. Place the fish on a rack set over a foil-lined tray, or use disposable foil broiling pans for easier cleanup. If you are broiling outdoors, you may wish to lightly oil the rack on which the fish will be laid. Broil the fish for 6–7 minutes, or until it is opaque and slightly browned around the edges. Flip the fish with a large metal spatula, and broil for 2–3 more minutes, until the fish is just cooked through.

4. Cut the lemon into 4 wedges, and serve each piece of fish with one of them. The Japanese typically serve a small mound of grated radish to the side of the fish. Each person then dribbles some soy sauce over the radish and spreads this mixture on the fish just before conveying it to the mouth. If you wish to follow suit, drain the grated radish of excess liquid before mounding it on the plates.

Fillets of Spanish mackerel (you can easily recognize their yellow-dotted silvery skin) are also wonderful when salt-grilled. Since they are usually not as thick as steaks, you'll probably find that they are done in 7–8 minutes total time. Score the skin with shallow slits, and grill the fish with the skin side to the source of heat for 2–3 minutes, then flip and cook until nearly done. Flip again and finish with a minute of cooking so that the skin is exposed to direct heat and becomes crisp.

Soused Grilled Black Cod
Tara no Kasu-Zuké

Serves 4

Keep this recipe in mind when you are shopping at your local fish market and you want to set aside something for later in the week. Black cod, found in the Pacific Northwest, is the fish of choice for *kasu-zuké* preparation. In fact, it was seeing ''*Kasu* Cod'' on the menu at Cafe Sport in Seattle, Washington, that reminded me of this dish that I had enjoyed so much while living in Japan. The recipe I've given here is an adaptation of the restaurant's version, with compliments of the chef, Tom Douglas.

> *4 small black cod steaks, about 3½ ounces each*
> *½ teaspoon coarse salt*

MARINADE:
> *1 cup* saké kasu *(lees; see the explanation here)*
> *¼ cup dark brown sugar, packed*
> *⅓–½ cup water*

1. Rinse the cod steaks under fresh cold water and pat them dry. Salt the fish evenly, all over.

2. Mash the lees and place them in a glass or ceramic container (I like to use a glass loaf pan). Add the brown sugar and water, and stir together to make a lumpy paste.

3. Push two thirds of the paste to the side, and smooth out the remaining third on the bottom of the container. Place two pieces of cod on the paste. Cover the cod pieces with half of the remaining mixture. Lay two more pieces of cod on top of the lees mixture, and cover the fish with the remaining lees paste.

Bluefish, which is abundant on the Atlantic coast, is very tasty when prepared in the kasu-zuké *manner, too. When broiling, expose the skin side of the fillet to the heat first, then flip and broil the flesh side. Depending upon the thickness of the fillet, bluefish will probably take only 3, or at most 4, minutes on each side.*

When saké *wine is made, the pasty lees, or* kasu, *that is a by-product of the fermenting process is kept and used as a pickling agent. It imparts a pleasantly winy aroma and tang to the vegetables and fish that are marinated in it. In the days before refrigeration, this kind of pickled food was eaten regularly throughout Japan. Even today, when it is no longer necessary, many Japanese still prefer the slightly fermented flavor of* kasu-zuké *to freshly caught catches.*

4. Cover the container snugly with clear plastic wrap, and allow the fish to marinate for at least 4 hours at a cool room temperature, or in the refrigerator for up to 24 hours.

5. Just before broiling, scrape off the lees paste (refrigerate it and reuse it up to three times within a month). Place the cod steaks on disposable foil broiling pans and broil 3–4 inches from the source of heat for 4–5 minutes. Flip the fish and broil for another 3–4 minutes, until golden and slightly crusty around the edges.

Snapper Grilled with Fragrant Pepper

Tai no Sansho Yaki

Snapper and sea bream belong to the group of fish called *tai* in Japanese, and since their name resembles the word *medetai* ("congratulations"), these fish are often served on happy occasions such as weddings. This method of grilling with fragrant pepper is one of my favorites.

Serves 2

2 pieces fillet of snapper, about 4–5 ounces each

1 tablespoon saké *(Japanese rice wine)*

1 teaspoon vegetable oil

½ teaspoon coarse salt

½ teaspoon dried sansho *(fragrant Japanese pepper)*

1 small lemon, cut into 4 wedges

1. Rinse the fillets under cold water, making sure that all scales have been removed from the skin. Remove any belly

bones with tweezers. Pat the fish dry. Marinate the fillets in the rice wine for 10 minutes, turning the fish once after 5 minutes. Pat the fillets dry again.

2. Lay the fillets, skin side up, on a disposable foil broiling pan. Lightly brush the skin with vegetable oil, then sprinkle it with half the salt and half the fragrant pepper.

3. Place the fish fillets under the broiler, skin side to the source of heat. Broil under intense heat for 2½–3 minutes. The skin will begin to blister a bit, and the edges of the fish will curl slightly and become opaque. Using a broad spatula, carefuly flip the fillets. Brush the flesh with a bit of oil and sprinkle the remaining salt and pepper on the fish.

4. Broil for 2–3 minutes, until the flesh becomes opaque and ever so slightly charred at the edges. Again using the broad spatula, carefully remove the fish to serving plates. Serve the fish hot, with lemon wedges on the side.

Golden-Glazed Scrod

Tara no Uni Yaki

Zesty sea urchin paste makes a shiny, golden glaze for firm and meaty scrod. The Japanese use a similar glaze on squid and monkfish, too.

Serves 4

    10–12 ounces scrod
    1 tablespoon saké *(Japanese rice wine)*
    ¼ teaspoon salt

GOLDEN GLAZE:

    1 tablespoon neri uni *(sea urchin paste)*
    1 large egg yolk
    1 teaspoon mirin *(syrupy rice wine)*

1. Cut the fish into four portions. Toss the fish with the rice wine, then sprinkle with the salt.

2. Place the fish on disposable foil broiling pans, and with the broiler turned up as high as it will go, broil the fish for 2–3 minutes, until opaque and barely cooked through.

3. In a small glass or ceremic bowl, combine the glaze ingredients and stir until very smooth. With a spoon, spatula, or clean pastry brush, apply the glaze to the fish. Return the fish to the broiler for 1 minute. Apply a second coating of glaze and broil for a final minute or more, until the glaze has dried somewhat and blistered ever so slightly. Serve immediately.

Broiled Air-Dried Pompano with Sesame

Mana-Gatsuo no Shōyu-Boshi

Serves 2

For centuries the Japanese have prepared oily fishes such as pompano and mackerel by marinating them in various combinations of soy and syrupy rice wine before drying them in the open air. This method of preparation seals in the flavor of the freshly caught fish, while extending its shelf life by several days. Although no longer necessary with modern refrigeration, succulent broiled air-dried fish remains one of the most popular dishes in Japanese homes today.

> *1 pompano, about 1 pound, filleted (fillets about 4 ounces each)*

MARINADE:

> *1 tablespoon soy sauce*
> *½ tablespoon mirin (syrupy rice wine)*

> *1 tablespoon white sesame seeds*
> *½ small lime, cut into 2 wedges*

1. With a sharp knife, make two or three shallow slits in the skin of the pompano over the thickest part of each fillet.

2. Combine the soy sauce and syrupy rice wine in a deep glass or ceramic dish, and marinate the fish, turning several times, for at least 2 hours, or up to 24 hours if refrigerated.

3. Remove the fish from the marinade (reserve the marinade for later), and place it skin side down on a flat rack, the kind you put cakes or cookies on to cool. I set my rack over a tray to catch any marinade drippings and place it in a cool spot out of direct sunlight. In my city apartment, that means the dining

room table. Allow the fish to air-dry for at least 2 hours and up to 5 or 6 hours, until the surface of the fish is dry to the touch and no longer sticky.

4. Paint the air-dried fish with some of the remaining marinade, and sprinkle the sesame seeds over the flesh side. Place the fish, skin side up, on a rack or disposable foil broiling pan. Preheat your broiler to the highest heat possible, and broil the fish 2–3 inches from the source of heat for 2 minutes. (The fish will begin to curl slightly.)

5. Turn the fish over and continue to broil for 5–6 minutes. The fish will be a glossy, burnished color, the sesame seeds toasted, and the surface ever so slightly charred in some places. Serve hot or at room temperature, with lime wedges.

Broiled Air-Dried Mackerel

Saba no Mirin-Boshi

Serves 3

Mackerel requires a slightly richer marinade than the air-dried pompano on page 182 and is best complemented by black sesame seeds and lemon wedges.

1 large mackerel, about 1½ pounds, filleted (fillets about 6 ounces each)

MARINADE:

   2 tablespoons soy sauce
   1 tablespoon saké *(Japanese rice wine)*
   2 tablespoons mirin *(syrupy rice wine)*

   1 tablespoon black sesame seeds
   ½ lemon, cut into 3 wedges

1. With a sharp knife, cut each of the fillets into three pieces. Make a shallow "x" in the skin of the mackerel over the thickest part of each piece of fish.

2. Combine the soy sauce, rice wine, and syrupy rice wine in a deep glass or ceramic dish, and marinate the fish, turning it

several times, for at least 3 hours, and up to 12 hours if refrigerated.

3. Remove the fish from the marinade (reserve the marinade for later), and place it skin side down on a flat rack, the kind you put cakes or cookies on to cool. I set my rack over a tray to catch any marinade drippings and place it in a cool spot out of direct sunlight. In my city apartment, that means the dining room table. Sprinkle the flesh side of the fillets with the black sesame seeds. Allow the fish to air-dry for at least 3 hours and up to 7 or 8 hours, until the surface of the fish is dry to the touch and no longer sticky.

4. Place the fish, skin side up, on a rack or disposable foil broiling pan. Preheat your broiler to the highest heat possible, and broil the fish 2–3 inches from the source of heat for 2 minutes. (The fish will begin to curl slightly and the flesh will lighten in color.)

5. Turn the fish over and continue to broil for 5–6 minutes. The fish will be a beautiful burnished color, with the surface ever so slightly charred in some places.

6. Serve two pieces for each serving, with lemon wedges on the side. Serve the fish hot, or let it cool to room temperature.

Glaze-Grilled Swordfish

Kajiki no Teriyaki

Serves 4

The word *teriyaki* means "glaze-grill," and it is a popular method of preparing fish and meat in Japan. Unlike many American versions of this dish, true *teriyaki* dishes are neither marinated in a heavy soy-based sauce nor are they baked and then drowned in a sweet soy gravy. Authentic *teriyaki* cooking involves a quick searing followed by a light napping with a sweetened soy sauce to produce a complex, layered effect—glossy, slightly crusty burnished exterior with a snowy white, moist, and tender interior. Sometimes glaze-grilling is done on an outdoor grill or under a broiler, and at those times the glaze is painted on the seared fish in several layers toward the end of the cooking process. With thick fish and meat steaks, though, glaze-grilling usually means searing the food in a heavy skillet, then braising it in a rapidly reducing sweetened soy glaze. Swordfish can be enjoyed either way.

SWEETENED SOY GLAZE:

> *4 tablespoons soy sauce*
>
> *3 tablespoons* mirin (*syrupy rice wine*)
>
> *1 tablespoon sugar*

> *4 pieces swordfish, each about 4–5 ounces and at least ½ inch thick*
>
> *3 tablespoons* saké (*Japanese rice wine*)
>
> *¼ teaspoon salt*
>
> *2 teaspoons vegetable oil*

1. In a small saucepan set over low heat, combine the glaze ingredients and stir constantly until the sugar is dissolved. Continue to cook the sauce for 3 minutes; it will become quite foamy and bubbly. Pour the sauce into a small heatproof glass jar or bowl, and let it sit until cool. (The glaze can be made up at your convenience and stored, covered, in the refrigerator for 2–3 weeks.)

2. When you are ready to cook, place the pieces of swordfish in a flat-bottomed glass dish and sprinkle the rice wine over them, turning the pieces so that all surfaces become moist. Let the fish sit for 5 minutes. Just before cooking, lightly salt both sides of each piece of fish.

3. To cook on an outdoor grill: Brush the fish very lightly with the oil, and sear the fish over hot coals for 2–3 minutes. Flip the fish and sear the other side for another 1½–2 minutes. While the second side is cooking, paint the first side (now facing up) with the glaze. Flip the fish and paint the other side with glaze. Cook for another minute. Flip and repaint the fish with glaze, cooking for another minute. A total of 7–8 minutes cooking time should be sufficient for swordfish about ¾ inch thick. Pour extra glaze over the fish when serving.

To cook in a skillet: Heat the oil in a heavy skillet over high heat. Sear the fish for 1½ minutes on each side. If your skillet is not large enough to accommodate all the fish at once, sear it in batches. Lower the heat slightly, and add half of the soy glaze to the empty pan, cooking it until bubbly. Return two pieces of the fish, and cook for 2 minutes. Flip the fish, raise the heat to high, and continue cooking for another minute. The sauce should be reduced to a richly colored glaze. Transfer the glazed fish to serving plates, and pour any remaining pan juices over the fish; keep these pieces warm. Quickly rinse out the pan, and repeat with the remaining soy glaze and seared fish.

Cattail-Seared Mackerel, City Style

Aji no Kabayaki, Machi Fū

Serves 2

Kabayaki, or "cattail-searing," is an ancient method of preparing eels in Japan. The name derives from the resemblance of a skewered, soy-glazed fillet of eel to a cattail growing in a marsh. Today, many Japanese make a home version of *kabayaki* with the more easily accessible and less costly mackerel. Most urban Japanese kitchens are equipped with a small but powerful broiling unit, and many people will grill directly over a gas fire. This method produces a fair amount of smoke, which the Japanese have come to expect and tend to ignore. When I tried making *kabayaki*-style mackerel in the traditional manner in my New York apartment, my neighbors were ready to call the fire department. Wanting to savor this flavorful fish dish more than just once a year at an outdoor barbecue, I adapted the method to what I call "city-style" grilling, using a skillet.

TARÉ SAUCE:

   4 tablespoons soy sauce

   1 tablespoon mirin *(syrupy rice wine)*

   2 tablespoons sugar

   1 mackerel, filleted, each fillet about 3½ ounces

   1 tablespoon vegetable oil

1. In a small saucepan, combine the *taré* sauce ingredients. Over low heat, cook while stirring to dissolve the sugar. Set aside.

2. Quickly rinse the mackerel fillets in cold water, then pat them dry.

3. Heat a cast-iron or other heavy-duty skillet over high heat. Pour the oil in and tilt the pan to coat it evenly.

4. Sear the mackerel fillets, skin side up, for 1 minute or until golden. Flip the fillets with a broad spatula, and sear them, skin side down, for another minute.

5. Press lightly against the fish with your spatula, and pour off all excess oil from the pan. Add the *taré* sauce, lower the heat, and cover the skillet. Allow the fish to braise for 1 minute. Flip, and repeat the braising for another minute, covered.

6. Remove the lid, return the heat to medium-high, and, shaking the pan, reduce the liquid to a richly colored glaze. Serve hot, or allow to cool to room temperature.

Cattail-Seared Eel on Rice

Unadon

Serves 2

Many marshes in Japan are filled with cattails, and the image of these plump, burnished brown aquatic grasses is appealing to the Japanese. So much so that glazed plank-grilled eels and other butterflied fishes that fan out to resemble the shape and color of cattails are called by that name.

If you've never eaten grilled eel before, you may be surprised at how rich yet finely textured the meat is. The sweet soy glaze helps seal in the natural oils and flavor. Excellent commercially prepared *kabayaki* ("cattail-seared" eel) is available at most Oriental groceries in the United States. Look in the freezer section where vacuum-sealed packages are stored. These make a quick, nutritious, and delicious meal.

EXTRA SAUCE *(if needed; see step 1)*:

   3 tablespoons soy sauce

   3 tablespoons mirin *(syrupy rice wine)*

   1 teaspoon sugar

   2 servings 3½ ounces each kabayaki *(glaze-grilled eel)*

   2 cups hot cooked rice (page 213)

   ¼ teaspoon sansho *(fragrant Japanese pepper)*

1. Check to see if your purchased eel comes with a packet of extra sauce. If it doesn't, make some for yourself: In a small saucepan combine the soy sauce, syrupy rice wine, and sugar. Cook, stirring, over medium heat until bubbly. Continue to simmer for 5–6 minutes, or until the sauce is reduced to a syrupy glaze.

2. Heat the glaze-grilled eel according to packet instructions. (This is usually in the original bag in a pot of simmering water, or in a microwave oven.)

3. Divide the hot rice between two deep bowls. Place the heated eel on top of the rice, and pour the extra sauce over all. Garnish with a sprinkling of fragrant pepper, and serve immediately.

Lemon-Broiled Sea Trout

Masu no Remon Yaki

Most Japanese homes have small kitchens with no oven, but with a broiler-like unit for stove-top cooking instead. The Japanese often broil fish on it for dinner. This recipe's technique combines skillet-searing with a final broiling, and is particularly well suited to cooking meaty fish fillets such as sea trout, rockfish, and tautog (blackfish).

Serves 2

1 fillet of sea trout, 10–12 ounces, skin still attached

MARINADE:

    2 tablespoons fresh lemon juice

    2 tablespoons saké *(Japanese rice wine)*

    ½ tablespoon vegetable oil

    2 teaspoons soy sauce

  6–8 thin slices lemon

1. Rinse the fish under cold water and pat dry. Cut the fillet into two pieces. Combine the lemon juice and rice wine in a

glass or other nonmetallic container, and marinate the fish, flesh side down, at room temperature for at least 30 minutes. (If you are refrigerating the fish, it should marinate for at least 1½ hours and up to 5 hours.)

2. Lift the fish from the marinade and pat it dry with paper towels. Heat the oil in a heavy skillet. Over medium-high heat sear the fish, flesh side down, for 1½ minutes. Flip the fish carefully with a spatula, and continue to cook over high heat for another minute.

3. Transfer the fish, skin side down, to a disposable foil broiling pan. Lightly paint the fish with soy sauce, then lay three or four lemon slices, slightly overlapping, on each piece of fish. Lightly paint the lemon slices with the soy sauce.

4. Place the fish under a preheated broiler and cook for 2 minutes, or until the lemon slices look lightly toasted. Flip the lemon slices over and paint them again with a bit more soy sauce. Broil for another 2–3 minutes. Carefully remove the fish with a broad spatula and serve, dribbling on a few more drops of soy if you like.

Fresh Tuna Steaks in Ginger Beurre Blanc

Maguro no Shōga An Kaké

Serves 2–3

Thanks to the proliferation of *sushi* bars in America, fresh tuna is now available in many fish markets. In addition to the usual *nigiri-zushi* (compact ovals of vinegared rice draped with slices of fresh fish) and *sashimi* (sliced fresh fish), Japanese chefs are experimenting with tuna in Continental-style preparations, too. This is a divine-tasting dish that pairs lean tuna with a rich and pungent ginger sauce.

6–8 ounces fresh tuna fillet

MARINADE:

> *¼ cup* saké *(Japanese rice wine)*
>
> *1 tablespoon ginger juice (extracted from grated fresh ginger)*

GINGER BEURRE BLANC:

> *1 tablespoon very finely minced shallot*
>
> *1 tablespoon peeled and very finely minced fresh ginger*
>
> *1 tablespoon rice vinegar*
>
> *2 tablespoons* saké *(Japanese rice wine)*
>
> *3–4 tablespoons sweet butter*
>
> *pinch salt*

GARNISH:

> *1–2 teaspoons finely chopped* beni shōga *(red pickled ginger)*

1. Rinse the fish under cold water and pat dry. Cut the fish into two or three portions. Combine the *saké* and ginger juice in a bowl, and marinate the fish, covered, in the mixture for

at least 30 minutes at room temperature, and up to several hours if refrigerated

2. Place the minced shallots and ginger in a small saucepan. Add the vinegar and rice wine, and bring to a boil. Reduce the heat and simmer 1 minute or until reduced by half. Remove the saucepan from the heat and whisk in the butter, a bit at a time, until the sauce thickens. Set the sauce aside while you cook the fish.

3. Lift the fish from the marinade, and pat it dry on paper towels. Lightly sprinkle the fish with salt. Place a non-stick skillet over fairly high heat, and sear the fish for 2 minutes. Flip the fish and continue to cook over high heat for another 2 minutes. The tuna steaks should be rare in the center.

4. Remove the tuna from the skillet to heated serving dishes. Pour the warm ginger beurre blanc sauce over the tuna, garnish with bits of red pickled ginger, and serve immediately.

Bay Scallop Sauté with Fiery Lime Sauce

Hotatégai no Sudachi Itamé

Serves 4

Japanese horseradish, called *wasabi*, is affectionately referred to as *namida*, or "tears," by many *sushi* bar aficionados. Here the *wasabi* is used to emblazon a delicate butter sauce, added to the scallops at the last moment. Neither *wasabi*'s aroma nor its fire will withstand exposure to high heat, so the sauce must be added just before serving.

FIERY LIME SAUCE:

  ¼ *stick (2 tablespoons) sweet butter, softened*

  2 *teaspoons* wasabi (*Japanese horseradish*) *powder*

  2 *teaspoons fresh lime juice*

  1 *pound bay scallops*

  1 *tablespoon* saké (*Japanese rice wine*)

  ⅛ *teaspoon salt*

  1–2 *teaspoons vegetable oil*

  1 *teaspoon fresh lime juice*

  1 *tablespoon soy sauce*

1. With a fork, whip the butter until light and fluffy. In a separate bowl, mix the horseradish powder with the lime juice to make a paste. Add the paste to the butter, whipping it in. Chill the seasoned butter.

2. Toss the scallops with the rice wine to moisten them. Sprinkle the salt over the scallops.

3. Heat a heavy skillet over a high flame. Lightly oil the skillet. Sauté the scallops over high heat for 1–1½ minutes, stirring frequently. Add the lime juice and sauté for another 30–40 seconds. Then add the soy sauce and sauté for yet another 30–40 seconds.

4. Remove the skillet from the heat. Add the chilled butter and stir as the butter melts to make the sauce. Serve immediately.

Soy-Simmered Sand Dabs

Ko Karei no Nitsuké

Serves 4

The classic Japanese presentation makes use of whole small flatfish called *ko karei*. The closest thing we have to them in America are the sand dabs caught off both east and west coasts. Sports fishermen often bring in these tasty tiny flatfish, and if you've caught some, this is the perfect way to enjoy them. Halibut steaks make a good substitute.

> *4 whole sand dabs, about 5–6 ounces each,* OR *4 small halibut steaks*

SIMMERING LIQUID:

> *1 strip (3–4 inches)* dashi kombu (*kelp for stock making*)
>
> *2 cups water*
>
> *¼ cup* saké (*Japanese rice wine*)
>
> *1 tablespoon sugar*
>
> *2 tablespoons* mirin (*syrupy rice wine*)
>
> *6 tablespoons soy sauce*
>
>
> *2 teaspoons cornstarch*
>
> *1½ teaspoons cold water*
>
> *large bunch radish sprouts* OR *watercress*

1. Wash the sand dabs well, removing their small, fine scales by scraping with the non-cutting edge of a knife. Gut each fish by slitting it just below the gills and pulling out and discarding the viscera. Rinse and pat dry. With a sharp knife, score the dark side of the skin of each fish in a diamond pattern.

If you are using halibut steaks, just rinse them and pat them dry.

2. In a wide shallow pot (or a deep wide skillet), combine the kelp and water over high heat. Remove the kelp when the water begins to bubble, and season the broth with the remaining simmering-liquid ingredients. Over low heat, simmer the liquid for 2–3 minutes, stirring occasionally to dissolve the sugar.

3. Line your pot or skillet with a dried bamboo leaf or cooking parchment (see note here). Press lining in place with liquid in pot. Carefully lay two sand dabs or halibut steaks on top, side by side, dark skin facing up for the whole fish. (If your pot is too small to accommodate two portions at a time, you'll need to repeat the simmering process three more times.)

4. Simmer the fish for 3–4 minutes. Ladle the gently bubbling liquid over the fish often as it simmers. The sand dabs will become firm, the decorative slits more pronounced, and the eyes opaque; the halibut steaks will lose their translucency and firm up. To remove the cooked fish, lift up the sling-like bamboo leaf or parchment. Carefully transfer each fish to an individual plate that has a rim (to accommodate a bit of sauce later). Cover with a lid or foil to keep the fish warm while you simmer the other portions.

5. Combine the cornstarch and cold water in a small cup to make a paste, and thicken the remaining simmering liquid with the cornstarch paste. Spoon this sauce over the fish just before serving.

6. Garnish with radish sprouts or sprigs of watercress.

The Japanese traditionally use dried bamboo leaves to line their pots when simmering fish. The bamboo leaves help keep the food from sticking to the pot and make removing the cooked fish later a lot easier. Bamboo leaves are usually packaged in bunches of 7–10 sheets. They are available in many Oriental grocery stores, and using them will add a nuance of woodsy flavor to the broth.

You can, however, use cooking parchment with equal success. You'll need a piece about 12 by 18 inches. Fold it in half lengthwise, to create a strip that is long enough to extend out of your pot or skillet on both sides.

Kelp is used to make most stocks in the Japanese kitchen. Although it does not have a distinctive flavor of its own, it helps enhance the flavors of other foods. Kelp left over from making this preparation can be used to make Fancy Kelp Knots (page 228) or to add a nuance of flavor to the rice used for sushi (page 49).

Soy-Simmered Shad Roe

Nishin no Ko no Nitsuké

Serves 2

Cod roe prepared this way is a prized delicacy in Japan. With our fresh shad roe, this dish is even better!

1 large shad roe, about 6 ounces

SIMMERING LIQUID:

1 strip (1–2 inches) dashi kombu (kelp for stock making)

1 cup water

2 paper-thin slices fresh ginger, each the size of a quarter

2 tablespoons saké (Japanese rice wine)

1 tablespoon sugar

1 tablespoon mirin (syrupy rice wine)

4 tablespoons soy sauce

2 teaspoons cornstarch

1 teaspoon cold water

1 tiny knob fresh ginger, the size of a nickel

The Japanese traditionally use dried bamboo leaves to line their pots when simmering delicate fish and roes. The bamboo leaves help keep the food from sticking to the pot and makes removing the cooked food later much easier. Bamboo leaves are usually packaged in bunches of 7–10 sheets. They are available in many Oriental grocery stores and using them will add a woodsy nuance of flavor to the broth. Cooking parchment makes a good substitute; you'll need a piece about 12 by 18 inches. Fold it in half, lengthwise, to create a strip that is long enough to extend from your pot or skillet on both sides.

Kelp is used to make most stocks in the Japanese kitchen. Although it does not have a distinctive flavor of its own, it helps enhance the flavors of other foods. Kelp left over from making this preparation can be used to make Fancy Kelp Knots (page 228) or to add a nuance of flavor to the rice used for sushi (page 49).

1. Rinse the roe carefully and gently pat it dry. With a sharp knife, split the roe in two.

2. In a wide shallow pot (or deep wide skillet), combine the kelp and water over high heat. Remove the kelp when the water begins to bubble, and season the broth with the remaining simmering-liquid ingredients. Over low heat, simmer the liquid for 1–2 minutes, stirring occasionally to dissolve the sugar.

3. Line your pot or skillet with a dried bamboo leaf or cooking parchment (see the note, on page 197). Press lining in place with liquid in the pot. Carefully lay the pieces of roe on top.

4. Simmer the roe for about 4–5 minutes, frequently ladling the gently bubbling liquid over it, until it is no longer pink. The roe will curl and ''blossom'' as the skin shrinks, exposing the eggs inside. To remove the cooked roe, lift up the sling-like bamboo leaf or parchment. Carefully transfer each piece to an individual serving plate.

5. Peel the knob of ginger, then slice it into tissue-thin slices. Stack these on each other and cut them into thread-like slivers. Soak these in a bowl of ice water for 1–2 minutes.

6. Combine the cornstarch and cold water in a small cup to make a paste. Thicken the remaining simmering liquid with the cornstarch paste, and spoon this sauce over each portion of roe. Drain the ginger threads, garnish each serving of roe with a portion of slivered ginger.

Bluefish Poached in *Miso*

Sakana no Miso Ni

Serves 2

Fermented bean paste, called *miso,* is used in many ways in the traditional Japanese kitchen. It is probably best known in the West as a thickener for soups, though its use in simmered and sauced dishes, such as this one, is also deeply rooted in Japan's culinary traditions. The final garnish of fresh ginger adds an extra measure of flavor.

NERI MISO SAUCE:

4 *tablespoons* aka miso (*dark fermented bean paste*)

3 *tablespoons sugar*

2 *tablespoons* saké (*Japanese rice wine*)

1 *fillet of bluefish, 8 to 10 ounces*

⅔ *cup* dashi (*basic sea stock, page 27*) OR *water*

1 *tiny knob fresh ginger, the size of a nickel*

1. Combine the fermented bean paste, sugar, and rice wine in a small saucepan, stirring to mix well. Cook the sauce for 3–4 minutes over a medium flame, stirring constantly as the sauce thickens and bubbles. Set the sauce aside.

2. Rinse the fish fillet, pat it dry, and then cut it into two pieces. Score the skin side with a few slashes (to keep the fish from curling when cooking).

3. Pour the sea stock or water into a skillet large enough to hold the two pieces of fish in a single layer. Remove the peel from the fresh ginger, and add the peel to the skillet.

4. Cut the peeled knob of fresh ginger into tissue-thin slices. Stack these, and then cut them into very fine threads. Soak

these ginger threads in cold water for a few minutes while you poach the fish.

5. Lay the fish, skin side down, in the skillet. Over medium-low heat, bring the liquid in the skillet to a gentle simmer. Poach the fish for 2–3 minutes, until the color changes and the flesh firms a bit. Spoon the simmering liquid over the fish often as it cooks.

6. Discard the ginger peel, add the *neri miso* sauce to the skillet, and stir to incorporate smoothly. Carefully flip the fish so that the skin faces up. Continue to poach the fish for another 2–3 minutes, until the sauce thickens and becomes glossy.

7. Drain the ginger threads. Using a broad spatula, transfer the fish to your serving plates, skin side down. Spoon extra sauce over the fish, then garnish with a pile of ginger threads.

Fresh Crab and Noodles in a Pot

Kani Nabé

Serves 4

In Hokkaido, the northernmost island of the Japanese archipelago, this one-pot meal is a midwinter treat. The same bubbling-pot preparation can become a showcase for American Dungeness crabs caught along the Pacific Northwest coast or for our blue crabs from the Eastern Shore. Since fresh *enokidaké* mushrooms are being cultivated in California now, and *shiméjitaké* mushrooms are being grown in Virginia, this Japanese classic can be transplanted into American homes!

2–4 *whole fresh crabs, about 1½ pounds in all*

12–20 *square inches* dashi kombu (*kelp for stock making*)

2 *cups cold water*

1 *tablespoon* saké (*Japanese rice wine*)

pinch salt

4–5 *scallions, white and green parts*

¼ *pound (about ¼ head)* hakusai (*Chinese cabbage*)

4–5 *ounces dried* harusamé (*cellophane noodles*)

3–4 *ounces* enokidaké (*slender creamy white*) OR shiméjitaké (*clusters of small pale brown*) *mushrooms*

2–3 *tablespoons soy sauce*

½ *lemon, cut into 4 wedges*

If live crabs are unavailable, use already blanched (cooked) crabs instead. Simmer them in the kelp broth for 1 minute before placing them on the platter of ingredients.

1. With a sharp heavy-duty cleaver, cut each crab in half through the belly (this kills them immediately), then cut off the legs. Using the tip of your knife, slit each leg (to facilitate eating later on).

2. In a small pot, combine the kelp and the water, and bring rapidly to a boil. Then remove the kelp and season the broth

with the rice wine and salt. Blanch the crab pieces in the seasoned broth for 2 minutes, or until the shells turn a vivid red. Remove the crabs to a platter, and skim the froth from the poaching liquid. Set the broth aside.

3. Trim the tops and bottoms from the scallions, then cut them into 2-inch lengths. Stack these bundles of scallions on the platter with the blanched crab pieces.

4. Cut the cabbage into 1½-inch lengths, and stack these near the crab on the same platter.

5. Soak the noodles in warm water for 10–15 minutes; drain, and place them on the platter too.

6. Trim away the bottom of the slender white mushrooms, or if you are using the pale brown ones, trim away any moldy material clinging to the stems before breaking the larger clusters into smaller ones. Add these to the platter of ingredients.

7. Bring the platter of ingredients to the table if you have a portable cooking unit, and make the bubbling pot there. If not, prepare it in the kitchen and then bring it to the table. Either way, begin by simmering the blanched crabs and noodles in the broth for 2–3 minutes. Then add the cabbage, and adjust the seasoning with the soy sauce. Cover the pot and let it simmer for 2–3 minutes. Add the scallions and mushrooms, and simmer another minute or 2. Serve piping hot, with lemon wedges on the side.

Bubbling Pot with Monkfish

Ankō Nabé

Serves 4

This dish combines the slight bitterness of broccoli rabe with the slight sweetness of monkfish in an aromatic *miso*-thickened broth. It's a wintertime dish in Japan—particularly popular in the northern prefectures.

> *1 pound monkfish fillet*
> *12–20 square inches dashi kombu (kelp for stock making)*
> *2 cups cold water*
> *1 tablespoon saké (Japanese rice wine)*
> *pinch salt*
> *½ pound broccoli rabe*
> *¼ pound (about ¼ head) hakusai (Chinese cabbage)*
> *4–5 ounces dried harusamé (cellophane noodles)*
> *4 large fresh shiitaké (dark oak) mushrooms*
> *½ tablespoon mirin (syrupy rice wine)*
> *3 tablespoons dark miso (fermented bean paste; preferably Sendai miso)*

1. Cut the monkfish fillet into 16–20 bite-size pieces. In a small pot, combine the kelp and the water, and bring the water rapidly to a boil. Remove the kelp, and season the broth with the rice wine and salt.

2. Poach the monkfish pieces in the seasoned broth for only 30 seconds, or until the fish turns opaque. Remove the fish to a platter. Skim the froth from the poaching liquid, and set the broth aside.

3. Wash the broccoli rabe well in cold water, trimming away any leaves that are not bright green. Tie the stalks together in several bunches. In a small pot of boiling water to cover,

The kelp used here can be recycled into Fancy Kelp Knots (page 228).

quickly blanch the broccoli rabe until it is bright green and just barely wilted, about 1 minute. Remove the bunches from the water with tongs or chopsticks, and transfer them immediately to a bowl of cold water. When the rabe is cool, remove it from the water and squeeze out all excess liquid. Cut off the tied stems, keeping the stalks in bundles. Cut the bundles in half lengthwise if they are more than 2 inches long. Stack these bundles of blanched rabe on the same platter as the poached fish pieces.

4. Cut the cabbage into 1½-inch lengths, and stack these near the blanched rabe.

5. Soak the noodles in warm water for 10–15 minutes; drain, and place them on the platter too.

6. Remove the stems from the *shiitaké* mushrooms, and add the stems to the fish poaching liquid. Gently simmer the broth for 5 minutes, then pick out the stems and discard them. Skim any froth from the broth, and season with the syrupy rice wine. Wipe the caps of the mushrooms with a damp cloth to remove any soil that might be clinging to them. Slice the caps in half diagonally, and set them on the platter with the fish, noodles, and vegetables.

7. Place the fermented bean paste on the platter with the other ingredients.

8. Bring the platter of ingredients to the table if you have a portable cooking unit, and make the bubbling pot there. If not, prepare it in the kitchen and then bring it to the table. Either way, begin by simmering the poached fish and noodles in the broth for 2–3 minutes. Then add the cabbage, whisk in the fermented bean paste, cover the pot, and let it gently bubble for 2 minutes. Add the *shiitaké* mushrooms, then the broccoli rabe, and simmer another minute or 2. Serve piping hot.

Seafood Dumpling Pot
Oden

Serves 2

In the cold months, vendors set up their snack stands on the side streets of Tokyo, Osaka, and other large cities late at night. Stone-roasted sweet potatoes, noodles in broth, and this slow-simmered seafood pot are the three most popular midnight-snack offerings. Try this stew on a chilly night with piping hot rice and a few pickled vegetables; it's guaranteed to warm you quickly.

2–3 *sticks* chikuwa (*roasted seafood sausage*), OR 4–6 satsuma agé (*deep-fried seafood patties*)

4 *boiling* (*not baking*) *potatoes, 3–4 ounces each*

5-inch piece of daikon (*Japanese white radish*), *about 4 ounces*

BROTH:

2½ *cups* dashi (*basic sea stock, page 27*)

2 *tablespoons* saké (*Japanese rice wine*)

2½ *tablespoons* usukuchi shōyu (*light soy sauce*)

1 *teaspoon salt*

1 *teaspoon* karashi (*hot Japanese mustard*) *powder, mixed with a scant teaspoon cold water*

If you buy a large package of chikuwa *and have some left over, try the pilaff on page 220. Or you can stuff the sausages with sticks of cucumber, or cooked string beans or asparagus, and cut them into ½-inch lengths. Stick a toothpick in each piece and serve them as hors d'oeuvres with some* wasabi-jōyu (*soy sauce mixed with* wasabi *horseradish*) *for a dip.*

1. Cut each stick of fish sausage into four pieces. Or cut the seafood patties in half. (If you are using the patties, quickly blanch them in boiling water to remove excess oil.) Peel the potatoes, and cut them in half if they are more than 2 inches thick. Peel the radish, and cut it into four rounds if less than 2 inches in diameter, or into thicker half-moon slices if the radish is large.

2. Combine the broth ingredients in a wide-mouthed shallow pot, and bring it to a boil. Lower the heat, and gently simmer the sausage, potatoes, and radish in the broth for 20–25 minutes, or until the vegetables are barely tender. Let the mixture stand in the pot for at least 30 minutes, or up to 24 hours if refrigerated.

3. Ten to 15 minutes before serving, slowly heat the sausage and vegetables in the broth.

4. Serve the stew piping hot in bowls. Either dab the sausage and vegetables with mustard as you eat, or dissolve a bit of mustard in the broth.

Hot-Stone Fish Stew

Ko Karei no Ishi Yaki Nabé

Serves 4

I first sampled this unusual dish at a traditional inn in Wajima, a city at the tip of the Noto Peninsula, which juts dramatically out into the Sea of Japan. Wajima is known for its exquisite lacquerware, and many of the plates used in serving the meal that day were lacquered wood.

But this grand bubbling pot was quite different. A huge sturdy ceramic bowl was brought to the table, filled with lightly grilled miniature sand dabs, slivers of *daikon* radish, bunches of bright green *nanohana* (a vegetable resembling broccoli rabe), and a scattering of brightly colored edible flowers in a *miso*-thickened broth. The chef proceeded to bury white-hot rocks in the broth, and immediately the stew began to bubble! Not only was the dish spectacular to behold, but the melding of flavors and textures was truly memorable.

> *8 small sand dabs, about 3½–4 ounces each, OR 2 halibut steaks, about 6 ounces each*
>
> *1 tablespoon* saké (*Japanese rice wine*)
>
> *½ teaspoon salt*
>
> *1 teaspoon vegetable oil, optional*
>
> *6–8 ounces* daikon (*Japanese white radish*)
>
> *1 large bunch broccoli rabe, about 5 ounces*

BROTH:

> *20 square inches* dashi kombu (*kelp for stock making*)
>
> *6 cups cold water*
>
> *1 tablespoon soy sauce*
>
> *1 tablespoon* mirin (*syrupy rice wine*)
>
> *¼ cup* shiro miso (*light fermented bean paste*)
>
> *8 edible flowers (squash blossoms are particularly pretty)*
>
> *3–4 clean smooth stones, each about 2 inches in diameter*

1. Scrape the scales off each sand dab; slit each belly open and clean it, but leave the head and tail intact. Rinse the fish and pat them dry. Moisten the fish with the rice wine, then sprinkle them with the salt.

You can either broil or grill the sand dabs. For a crisper texture, or if you think they might stick to an outdoor grill, dip a pastry brush in vegetable oil and lightly paint the sand dabs before broiling or grilling. Two minutes on each side should be sufficient to barely cook the fish and attractively char the surface. (This can be done several hours ahead, even the previous day, and refrigerated.)

If you are using halibut, cut each steak in half, then moisten them with the rice wine, sprinkle with salt, and broil.

2. Peel the radish, then cut it into 1½- to 2-inch-long sticks, each the thickness of a pencil.

3. Rinse and trim the broccoli rabe. Cut the stems into 1-inch lengths. Bring a pot of water to a rolling boil, add the broccoli rabe, and remove the pot from the heat. Stir, then drain immediately. Allow the rabe to cool to room temperature naturally. (This may be done hours ahead.)

4. Make the broth: Place the kelp in a pot with the cold water, and bring it to a rapid boil over high heat. Remove the pot from the heat, season the broth with the soy sauce and syrupy rice wine, then whisk the bean paste into the broth. Discard the kelp, and strain the broth into a 2-quart container. (This broth can be made several hours ahead, even the day before, and refrigerated.)

5. Fill the casserole: Alternate radish sticks and bunches of broccoli rabe on the bottom, then lay the lightly broiled or grilled fish over the vegetables. Just before bringing the casserole to the table, pour the broth over the fish and vegetables, and scatter the flowers over all.

 209

6. Heat the stones in a barbecue, outdoor pit, or even a home oven. It should take no more than 30 to 40 minutes at 500 degrees to make the stones hot enough to "cook" the stew.

7. Bring the hot stones to the table and add them to the broth with tongs. The broth will begin to bubble and steam immediately. Allow the stones to cook the stew for 4–5 minutes before dishing out the fish and vegetables moistened with broth. The leftover broth makes a delightful soup that the Japanese eat with white rice and pickled vegetables.

Tributary Treasures

Hot and cold side dishes, including seafood pilaffs, vegetable and seafood combinations, and several sea vegetable dishes

Basic Boiled Rice

Gohan

The Japanese serve unseasoned, unadorned short-grained rice with nearly every meal. Its subtle flavor is the perfect foil for other more complex dishes. The chart that follows shows the amount of fresh cold water needed to cook various quantities of raw rice. (The yield of cooked rice is about double the raw rice used.) It is extremely difficult to cook less than 1 cup of raw rice, and I recommend making 1½ cups or more at a time. Leftover rice responds well to freezing and microwave-reheating.

raw rice	cold water
1 cup	1 cup plus 2 tablespoons
1¼ cups	scant 1½ cups
1½ cups	1¾ cups
1¾ cups	2 cups plus 2 tablespoons
2 cups	2⅓ cups

1. Place the rice in a bowl and cover it with cold water. Stir the rice vigorously; the water will become cloudy with starch from the rice grains. Strain the rice, discarding the cloudy water, and repeat the washing procedure with fresh cold water. Continue to rinse, swish, and strain until the rinsing water runs clear.

2. Drain the washed rice well after the final rinsing. You will notice that the rice has become slightly more opaque; the kernels have begun to absorb moisture from the washing process, and this will ensure tender cooked rice.

3. Place the rice in a sturdy straight-sided pot. For a single cup of rice use a 2-quart pot; for 2 cups of raw rice a 3- to 3½-quart capacity is best. Measure in the indicated amount of fresh cold water. Cover the pot with a tight-fitting lid.

The Japanese have always prized the freshly harvested rice crop that comes to market in the fall; most Japanese willingly pay a premium for shin mai (''new rice''). In recent years, California has begun to market its Japanese-style short-grained ''new rice'' here in America, and happily at the same price as the storage crop. During the months of October and November, ask your nearest Japanese food store if they have shin mai. If they do, you're in for a treat.

Washing procedures remain the same, but shin mai requires less water for cooking. During October and November, equal quantities of rice and water should be just right. If you still have some shin mai left to cook in December, it's best to take a middle-of-the-road reading: Every cup of raw rice should be cooked with 1 cup plus 1 tablespoon cold water. By the beginning of the new year, all the rice sold in the stores will be storage crop and should be cooked according to the adjacent chart.

4. Over high heat, bring the water to a rolling boil. It's best not to remove the lid to check on the progress. Instead, rely on other clues: You can hear bubbling noises and see the lid begin to dance when the water boils. (This should take from 3 to 5 minutes.)

5. Reduce the heat and continue to cook until the water is absorbed (about 5 minutes). Again, rely on sound: You will hear a low hissing sound when it is done. If you must check, peek quickly, replacing the lid immediately.

6. Increase the heat to high again for 30 seconds, to dry off the rice. Remove the pot, still tightly covered, from the heat and let the rice stand for at least 10 minutes. Even if you wish to serve the rice piping hot, these final minutes of self-steaming are necessary to achieve the proper texture.

Rice Triangles with Ocean Confetti

Omusubi

The Japanese take the versatility of rice as a picnic food for granted, since they enjoy eating rice at room temperature, molded into a number of attractive shapes. These triangular sandwich-like rice bundles, garnished with a savory sprinkling of sea herbs and sesame, are packed for many a journey, hike, and school outing in Japan.

Makes 6

2 cups cooked rice (page 213), still warm

scant ¼ teaspoon salt

3–4 tablespoons Ocean Confetti (page 217)

1. If you will be packing the rice for a picnic, it's particularly important to salt it right after it has been cooked, as this acts as a preservative. Sprinkle the salt over the rice and toss lightly to mix well.

2. Divide the rice into six portions. With either your hands or a special *musubi-gata* mold, shape the rice into triangles.

Shaping with your hands: Keep your hands damp with cold water to prevent the rice from sticking to them. Compress the rice into a tight ball, and flatten the ball slightly. Moisten your hands again. Cup one hand to form a "roof" (upside-down V shape), and hold the other open to form a flat foundation. Squeeze the rice ball gently. Turn the rice, corner

Musubi gata *molds are a great convenience. They are sold in many Oriental groceries—the most common kind is made of cream-colored plastic. The molds should be washed by hand with warm water and a mild detergent. Do not put them in a dishwasher.*

by corner, to compress each of the three corners, making a perfect triangle. Repeat to make six triangles in all.

Shaping with a mold: Separate a *musubi-gata* mold into its two parts: a lid and a bottom, each in the shape of a double triangle. The bottom portion has holes in the sides of each triangle. Dip both pieces in cold water, and lay the bottom on your work board. Fill each triangle with a portion of rice; press the rice in firmly and evenly. Lift the lid piece from the cold water, and fitting it into the bottom, compress the rice inside. Remove the lid, invert the bottom, and tap the bottom to unmold the rice. If there is a problem, gently poke your fingers through the holes in the sides of the mold to help release the rice. Repeat to make six triangles in all.

3. Decorate either the tops or the sides with Ocean Confetti. Serve immediately, or wrap each triangle snugly in clear plastic wrap. The salted, molded rice will keep well at room temperature for 5–6 hours.

Ocean Confetti
Furikaké

Bits of sea herbs, toasted sesame, and smoky flaked fish make a delightful and nutritious seasoning mixture for plain boiled rice—frugal, too, since it makes use of leftovers from stock making.

Makes 1/3–1/2 cup, about 12 servings.

> *1 tablespoon white sesame seeds*
>
> *1/3–1/2 cup leftover* katsuo bushi (*dried bonito flakes; see note below*)
>
> *1 teaspoon soy sauce, optional*
>
> *1 teaspoon* mirin (*syrupy rice wine*), *optional*
>
> *1–2 teaspoons* ao nori (*sea herb flakes*)

1. Place the sesame seeds in a clean dry skillet and dry-roast them over medium-high heat for about 1 minute, or until just turning a golden brown. Shake the pan as you roast to ensure even coloration. Set the seeds aside in a small bowl.

2. Fish flakes that are left over from making seasoned stocks and sauces will need no further seasoning—just place the fish flakes in a large skillet with a non-stick surface. However, if your fish flakes are left over from making Basic Sea Stock, you will need to season them with the soy sauce and syrupy rice wine.

3. Over very low heat so as not to scorch the food, cook the fish flakes until they are dry. Stir constantly to separate any lumps or clumps. It could take as long as 10–15 minutes to accomplish this. Transfer the fish flakes to the bowl with the sesame seeds.

Leftovers from Smoky Sea Stock (page 28) and tempura dipping sauce (page 159), are preferable to flakes from Basic Sea Stock (page 27).

4. Add the sea herb flakes to the skillet, and gently shake over low heat for less than 1 minute; a wonderful sea aroma

will be evident. Transfer the flakes to the bowl with the sesame and fish flakes.

5. Stir the mixture of sesame, fish flakes, and sea herbs. Store it in an airtight container away from light, heat, and moisture until ready to use. It will keep fresh for 4–5 days on the shelf in cool weather, up to a month refrigerated. If you refrigerate the mixture, you may want to dry-roast it in a clean, dry non-stick skillet for a few seconds just before using it.

Rice with Savory Oysters, Japanese Style
Kaki Gohan

Serves 4–6

The Japanese often make a meal out of a flavored rice dish by adding a *miso* soup and some pickled vegetables to the menu. You could also serve this oyster and rice pilaff as an accompaniment to a poultry or meat entrée.

1½ *cups raw short-grained rice*

1 *strip* (2–3 *inches*) dashi kombu (*kelp for stock making*)

½ *cup water*

8–10 *oysters, about 8–10 ounces, shucked but in their natural liquor*

2 *tablespoons* saké (*Japanese rice wine*)

1 *tablespoon* usukuchi shōyu (*light soy sauce*)

1–1¼ *cups* dashi (*basic sea stock, page 27*)

1 *slender scallion, green part only*

2 *sprigs parsley*

1. Wash the rice until the water runs clear, then drain it well.

2. In a small saucepan, combine the kelp, water, oyster liquor, and rice wine, and bring it to a simmer. Poach the oysters in the seasoned liquid until they just barely firm up, about 1 minute. Strain the liquid through a cloth- or paper-lined strainer into a measuring cup, and set the oysters aside.

3. Season the strained liquid with the light soy sauce, and add enough sea stock to make 1¾ cups. Place this liquid with the washed and drained rice in a straight-sided 2-quart pot with a lid that fits snugly.

4. Cook the rice over high heat for about 5–6 minutes, or until you hear the liquid in the pot boiling furiously. The lid may begin to dance about and some foam may even escape. Lower the heat to maintain a steady but not especially strong boil.

5. Continue to cook the rice over a medium-low flame for another 6–7 minutes, or until all the liquid has been absorbed.

6. Remove the pot from the heat, toss in the blanched oysters, place a thin cloth or tea towel over the pot, and replace the lid immediately. Allow the oysters and rice to self-steam for 10–12 minutes.

7. Finely mince the green part of the scallion and the parsley; scatter this over the rice and toss in. The rice on the bottom of the pot is usually more colored by the soy-seasoned stock than that on the surface, so mix and toss to distribute evenly. Eat hot, warm, or cooled to room temperature.

Seafood Pilaff, Japanese Style
Umi no Sachi Gohan

Serves 4

Here, bits of seafood sausage and vegetables are cooked with rice to make a delicious accompaniment for almost any entrée. I like to make a large pot of this pilaff and then use the leftovers as poultry stuffing or filling for an omelet.

1½ *cups raw rice*

3–4 *sticks* chikuwa *(roasted seafood sausage)*

1 *small carrot*

3–4 *large button mushrooms*

1¾ *cups* dashi *(basic sea stock, page 27)* OR *water*

1 *tablespoon* mirin *(syrupy rice wine)*

1½ *tablespoons soy sauce*

2 *tablespoons finely chopped scallions, green part only*

1 *teaspoon* ao nori *(sea herb flakes), optional*

1. Wash the rice well until the water runs clear. Drain, and set aside.

2. Cut the seafood sausage in half lengthwise, then across into thin crescents. You should have about ¾ cup.

3. Peel the carrot and cut it in half lengthwise. Slice the carrot into thin half-circles. You should have about ⅓ cup.

4. Wipe the mushroom caps to remove any soil. Cut each mushroom in half, then across into thin slices. You should have about ⅓ cup.

5. In a small saucepan, combine the sea stock with the syrupy rice wine and soy sauce. Simmer the fish sausage and

vegetables in this mixture for 5 minutes. Strain, and reserve the cooking liquid, adding water or more stock if necessary to measure 1¾ cups. Set aside the sausage and vegetables.

6. Combine the washed and drained rice with the reserved cooking liquid in a 2- or 3-quart pot. Cover, and cook over high heat until the liquid begins to bubble, about 5 minutes. Adjust the heat to maintain a steady but not very vigorous boil, then continue to cook, covered, until all the liquid has been absorbed, about 5 minutes more.

7. Quickly toss in the simmered sausage and vegetables, and stir to distribute well. Re-lid the pot immediately and let it stand, self-steaming, for another 10–15 minutes.

8. Just before serving, sprinkle the rice with the scallions. If you want to add an extra sea aroma, sprinkle with sea herb flakes over it too. Serve hot or at room temperature.

Eggplant and Seafood Fry, Hakata Style

Hakata Ori Agé

Serves 4–6

Hakata is a city in Fukuoka Prefecture, famous for its *obi* sashes and *kimono* cloth woven in a striped pattern. Foods that appear to be striped are often called *hakata ori,* which means "woven in the Hakata style." Here the alternating layers of seafood and eggplant form the striped design. I often serve this dish with an American standby such as a fluffy omelet.

4 long, slender Oriental eggplants, about 12 ounces in all, with smooth, bright, blemish-free skin

SEAFOOD PASTE:

5 ounces scallops

3 ounces scrod, cut into small pieces

2 teaspoons shiro miso (*light fermented bean paste*)

1 small egg white

2 teaspoons cornstarch

2 teaspoons saké (*Japanese rice wine*)

1 teaspoon cornstarch

vegetable oil for deep-frying

½ lemon, cut into wedges

soy sauce for dipping, optional

1. Slice away the stem end of the eggplants, and use the piece to rub the cut edges together in a circular motion. The Japanese believe that this helps to rid eggplant of some of its bitterness; so do I. Rinse the eggplants. Trim off the pointed tips of the eggplants; save these for use in testing the

temperature of the oil later. Slice each eggplant lengthwise into three pieces. Lightly score the cut surfaces. Soak these pieces in cold water while preparing the seafood paste.

2. Place the scallops and scrod in the bowl of a food processor fitted with the metal blade. Pulse/process to blend. Add the bean paste and pulse/process again. Add the egg white and pulse/process to form a smooth paste. Mix the cornstarch with the wine, add the mixture to the seafood paste, and pulse/process to incorporate well.

3. Drain the eggplant slices and pat them dry with paper towels. Lightly dust the cut surfaces with a bit of cornstarch. Divide the seafood mixture into eight portions, and with a butter knife, spread a single portion on each of the eight end pieces (one side covered with purple skin, the other side not).

4. Assemble the eggplants by reconstructing the layers, placing a center slice between two end ones spread with seafood paste.

5. Heat the oil to about 370 degrees. Test with the tip ends of the eggplants; They should sink ever so slightly, rise immediately, and sizzle on the surface, coloring slowly. Deep-fry the stuffed eggplants, two at a time. Fry for about 3 minutes, turning once or twice during that time. (You can test for doneness by spearing the center with a sharp toothpick; it should come out clean.) Drain the eggplants and cut each into three or four segments, each about 1½ inches long.

6. Serve three or four segments per portion, with a lemon wedge. Some Japanese prefer to serve fried foods like these with *ponzu,* a dipping sauce made of equal parts of citron (lemon) juice and soy sauce.

Seafood-Stuffed Zucchini Baskets

Zukkīni no Surimi-Zumé

Serves 3–4

American summer gardens are often overrun by a bountiful zucchini crop. Here is another, and quite different, way of using that bounty. Serve these seafood-filled "baskets" with grilled chicken or steaks, or by themselves as part of a buffet or picnic basket.

> *3 slender, straight zucchini with bright, blemish-free skin*
>
> *1 teaspoon cornstarch*

SEAFOOD PASTE:

> *2–3 large shrimp, about 3 ounces in their shells*
>
> *3 ounces bay scallops*
>
> *1 teaspoon* shiro miso (*light fermented bean paste*)
>
> *2 teaspoons* saké (*Japanese rice wine*)
>
> *2 teaspoons cornstarch*

> *vegetable oil for deep-frying*
>
> *½ lemon, cut into wedges*
>
> *soy sauce for dipping, optional*

1. Slice away the stem end of the zucchini, and use the piece to rub the cut edges together in a circular motion. This is the Japanese method of eliminating some of the vegetable's bitterness. Rinse away the white foam that forms. Trim off the other end of each zucchini. Cut each zucchini into four or five 1½- to 2-inch lengths, for a total of 12–15 segments.

2. Using a melon baller, scoop out the seeds from each segment of zucchini, being careful not to poke a hole through

the bottom. Lightly dust the inside of the scooped-out zucchini "baskets" with cornstarch.

3. Peel and devein the shrimp; cut them into small pieces. Place the shrimp and scallops in the bowl of a food processor fitted with the metal blade. Pulse/process to blend. Add the bean paste and pulse/process again. Mix the cornstarch with the rice wine, add this to the seafood paste, and pulse/process to incorporate well.

4. Fill the scooped-out portion of each zucchini basket with the seafood mixture. Pack it smoothly and level with the top.

5. Heat the oil in a deep-fryer or wok to about 370 degrees. Test with a bit of the seafood mixture: It should sink ever so slightly, rise immediately, then sizzle and puff slightly on the surface, coloring slowly. Deep-fry the stuffed zucchini, three or four at a time. Fry for about 1½ minutes, turning once or twice during that time. (You can test for doneness by spearing the center with a sharp toothpick; it should come out clean.) Drain the zucchini well.

6. Serve three to five baskets per portion, with a lemon wedge. Some Japanese prefer serving fried foods with *ponzu*, which is a sauce made from equal parts of citron (lemon) juice and soy sauce.

If you like, save the scooped-out center portions of the zucchini and skewer them on toothpicks, two balls to each. Deep-fry the skewers for 1½ minutes. Serve with ponzu dipping sauce, made from equal parts of citron (lemon) juice and soy sauce.

Smoky Spinach Bundles

Hōrensō no Ohitashi

Serves 3–4

In Japan spinach is flat-leafed, not curly, and is never used raw in salads. Instead it is ever so briefly blanched, then dressed in a variety of sauces. The recipe here, called *ohitashi*, is for blanched spinach bundles, marinated in a seasoned smoky stock. The garnish, which looks a bit like brown sugar dusted on the top, is made from smoky fish flakes and sesame seeds.

1 large bunch spinach, about 8–10 ounces

¾ cup Tosa dashi (*smoky sea stock, page 28*)*, cooled*

2 tablespoons katsuo bushi (*dried bonito flakes*)

1 tablespoon white sesame seeds

1. Soak the spinach in a large tub of cold water, to remove all sand and gritty material. Cut two or three 10- to 12-inch lengths of kitchen twine, and lay one on the counter. Divide the spinach into two or three bunches with all the stems facing in the same direction. Use the twine to tie up the bunches of stems.

2. Bring a wide-mouthed pot of lightly salted water to a rolling boil. Place a single bunch of tied spinach in the pot, and with tongs or chopsticks, swish the bundle until the leaves are just wilted and bright green. Transfer the bundle, still tied with twine, to a bowl of ice water. Repeat the blanching procedure for the remaining bundles.

3. Rinse the cooled spinach bundles under fresh cold running water, and squeeze out all excess water.

4. Pour the sea stock into a glass loaf pan. Lay the spinach (still in bundles) in the stock, spreading out the leaves so that

all the spinach is barely submerged in the stock. Let the spinach sit in the stock for at least 15 minutes or up to several hours.

5. In a clean, dry skillet, dry-roast the fish flakes over high heat for 20–30 seconds. Empty them onto a clean, dry cloth (a handkerchief is fine). Pick up the ends of the cloth to enclose the flakes, and rub the flakes to make a coarse powder. Transfer the powder to a small bowl.

6. Dry-roast the sesame seeds in the same skillet for 40 seconds. Empty the seeds onto a clean, dry cutting board, and with a sharp knife, mince the seeds as you would parsley. Add the minced seeds to the fish powder.

7. Lift the spinach out of the sea stock, and squeeze out all excess liquid. Trim away the stems and twine. Cut the spinach leaves into 1½-inch lengths, and stack several lengths together to make three or four bundles. Serve chilled or at room temperature, garnished with a generous dusting of the fish and sesame mixture.

Fancy Kelp Knots
Musubi Kombu

*Makes 3 dozen, 12
to 18 servings*

As you've seen in this book, *dashi kombu,* or sturdy kelp, is used to season many stocks and broths in the traditional Japanese kitchen. In some frugal households, the kelp is used a second or third time to make a weaker broth. Personally, I find those secondhand stocks insipid, and I prefer to recycle my used kelp as a vegetable.

These nutritious fancy knots have a faint anise-like taste and are often added to a picnic of rice triangles (see page 215) or used to garnish a platter of grilled or fried fish or chicken.

36–40 *square inches softened* dashi kombu (*kelp left over
    from stock making*)

4–6 *tablespoons rice vinegar* (*to soften, not season, the
    kelp*)

2 *tablespoons water*

2 *tablespoons* saké (*Japanese rice wine*)

1 *tablespoon sugar*

3–4 *tablespoons soy sauce*

1. Cut the kelp into thirty-six strips, each ¼ inch wide and about 3 inches long. Tie each of these strips into a knot.

2. In a glass or enamel-lined pot, bring 2 or 3 cups of water to a rolling boil. Add 2–3 tablespoons of vinegar, and reduce the heat to maintain a steady but not vigorous boil. Add the kelp knots and cook for 8–10 minutes.

3. Drain the kelp knots, but do *not* refresh them under cold water. Fill the same saucepan with 2–3 cups fresh cold water and return it to a boil. Add the remaining 2–3 tablespoons vinegar, lower the heat slightly, and cook the kelp knots again, this time for 5–6 minutes. (Precooking the kelp in these acidulated baths helps tenderize the fibrous vegetable.) Drain the kelp knots.

4. Rinse the pot out and add the 2 tablespoons each of water and rice wine. Bring to a boil, reduce the heat slightly, and add the kelp knots. Cook for 3–4 minutes, then add the sugar. Stir frequently until the sugar has dissolved. Cook for another minute or 2, then add the soy sauce. The sauce will become foamy and will reduce rapidly. It is best to use an *otoshi-buta*, or "dropped lid," when simmering the kelp knots in the sweetened soy broth.

5. Being careful not to scorch the knots, cook them until they are well glazed and little or no sauce remains, about 5 minutes. Allow the kelp to cool in the cooking pan.

An otoshi-buta *or "dropped lid" is found in nearly every Japanese kitchen. Made from a cedar-like wood, it is slightly smaller than the circumference of the pot in which it is used. Instead of resting on the rim of the pot, the lid rests directly on the food inside. Particularly useful when simmering or braising with just a bit of liquid, it keeps the food moist while allowing the liquid to reduce and intensify slowly. The bubbling liquid hits against the inside of the lid during the cooking process and flavors and colors the top surfaces as well as the bottom. Sold in many Oriental groceries throughout America, buy a size ½–1 inch smaller than the diameter of your pot. Since the lids are made of wood, it is best to wash them with mild soap and warm water and let them dry naturally.*

Tricolored Sea Sauté

Hijiki no Itamé Ni

Serves 4–6

This colorful and nutritious mélange of land and sea vegetables is particularly good with broiled fish or poultry. Best savored at room temperature, it travels well in picnic baskets and is also excellent with cold cuts on a buffet table.

> ⅓ cup dried hijiki (*black sea vegetable*)
>
> 1 slender carrot, about 2 ounces
>
> 2 ounces slender green beans
>
> ½ tablespoon vegetable oil
>
> ¾ cup dashi (*basic sea stock, page 27*)
>
> 1 tablespoon saké (*Japanese rice wine*)
>
> 1½ tablespoons sugar
>
> ¼–⅓ cup soy sauce
>
> ½ tablespoon mirin (*syrupy rice wine*)
>
> 1 tablespoon white sesame seeds

Dried vegetables, both land and sea varieties, need to be softened first in warm water and then cooked slowly. In seasoning the cooking liquid, the Japanese first add softening agents such as wine and sugar; then toward the end they add soy sauce, which tends to "tighten" the foods. A final touch of syrupy rice wine both glazes and mellows the dish. For maximum flavor and texture, follow these instructions— don't add all the seasonings and stock at once.

1. Soak the dried sea vegetable in warm water for 20–30 minutes. Drain, and if necessary, cut the strands of *hijiki* to approximately ¾ inch long. Set the vegetable aside.

2. Peel the carrot and cut it into thin julienne strips about the same length as the sea vegetable pieces; set them aside.

3. Trim the green beans, and blanch them for 1 minute in boiling water to cover. Drain immediately, and let them cool to room temperature naturally. Slice the green beans on the diagonal into ¾-inch-long pieces, and set them aside.

4. Heat the oil in a skillet, and sauté the sea vegetable over high heat, stirring constantly, for 2 minutes. Add the carrot strips and continue to sauté for another minute.

5. Lower the heat, add ⅓ cup of the sea stock and the rice wine, and simmer for 6–7 minutes.

6. Add the sugar and ⅓ cup more stock. Stir, and simmer for 6–7 more minutes.

7. Add the soy sauce and remaining sea stock. Stir, and simmer for 7–8 minutes, or until the liquid is reduced to less than 1 tablespoonful.

8. Add the syrupy rice wine, stir, and return to high heat. Cook for another minute or so, until all the liquid has been reduced and the vegetables look glossy. Toss in the blanched string beans, and stir to mix. Remove the skillet from the heat, and let the sauté cool to room temperature.

9. In a small dry skillet, toast the sesame seeds for 30 seconds or so, until they color ever so slightly and a few pop. Just before serving, garnish the sea sauté with the sesame seeds.

Black and White Salad

Hijiki no Shira Aé

Serves 4–6

This soy-simmered black *hijiki* dressed in a creamy white *tōfu* sauce is both nutritious and tasty. Found on Japanese restaurant menus and home tables, Black and White Salad is particularly good when served with broiled or fried fish.

> ¼ *cup dried* hijiki (*black sea vegetable*)
> ½ *tablespoon vegetable oil*
> ⅔–¾ *cup* dashi (*basic sea stock, page 27*)
> 1 *tablespoon* saké (*Japanese rice wine*)
> *scant tablespoon sugar*
> 3 *tablespoons soy sauce*

DRESSING:

> ½ *cake* tōfu (*bean curd*), *about 2 ounces*
> 2 *tablespoons white sesame seeds*
> ½ *teaspoon* mirin (*syrupy rice wine*)
> 1 *teaspoon* usukuchi shōyu (*light soy sauce*)
> 1 *teaspoon rice vinegar*
> *pinch salt*

1. Soak the dried sea vegetable in warm water to cover for 20–30 minutes. Drain, and set aside.

2. Heat the oil in a skillet, and sauté the sea vegetable over high heat, stirring constantly, for 2 minutes. Lower the heat, add ¼ cup of the sea stock and the rice wine, and simmer for 6–7 minutes. (To achieve maximum flavor and best texture from the *hijiki*, it is important to cook this sea vegetable slowly, adding the wine, sugar, and soy in that order, bit by bit.)

3. Add the sugar and ¼ cup more stock. Stir, and simmer for 6–7 minutes. Add the soy sauce and a few more spoonfuls of sea stock. Stir, and simmer for 7–8 minutes, or until the liquid is completely reduced and the sea vegetable looks glossy. Taste a piece; it should be tender, with a faint licorice flavor. If the sea vegetable seems tough, add a bit more stock and simmer for an additional 3–5 minutes. Remove the skillet from the heat, and let the sauté cool to room temperature.

4. Blanch the bean curd in boiling water to cover for 1 minute, then drain. When it is cool enough to handle, place the bean curd in a fine-meshed cloth and squeeze out all moisture, mashing the bean curd to a smooth paste. Transfer the paste to a bowl.

5. In a small dry skillet, toast the sesame seeds for 30–40 seconds, until they color ever so slightly and a few pop. Transfer the seeds to a clean, dry cutting board, and mince the sesame as you would parsley. Add the minced seeds to the bean curd paste.

6. Season the bean curd mixture with the syrupy rice wine, light soy sauce, vinegar, and pinch of salt. Mix well. Drain the cooked sea vegetable, and pat away excess liquid with paper towels. Toss the drained sea vegetable in the white dressing, and mix well. Serve in small mounds, at room temperature or chilled.

A Peek in the Pantry

Special Japanese Ingredients

A glossary of Japanese ingredients called for in the recipes, with information on purchasing and storing

S hopping for unfamiliar Japanese ingredients can often be confusing, particularly since labeling is not always consistent, complete, clear, or in English. The listing that follows contains information on the Japanese foodstuffs you'll encounter in the recipes in this book—I hope you'll find it a useful guide when preparing a shopping list or working in your kitchen.

When you shop in person or order through a catalogue:

1. Let the clerk or mail-order house know what it is you want to make with the product. Some products are labeled generically, like "seaweed" or "bean paste," and not every kind of "seaweed" or "bean paste" is necessarily suitable for your purpose.

2. Whenever possible, refer to the item you want by using the Japanese name for it. English translations for the same product vary tremendously. There are also variations in the spelling of certain Japanese words—such as *konbu* and *kombu*, which are the same kelp. And occasionally products are given unnecessarily obscure names, such as "alimentary paste" instead of "noodles."

3. Many recipes using Japanese food products do not take into consideration the difference in size between an American

and a Japanese measuring cup. That difference is considerable: A Japanese cup is about ⁴⁄₅ the size of its American counterpart. Teaspoon and tablespoon measurements, though, are the same. All recipes in this book use standard American measures.

4. The freshness of a product is crucial, even when buying a dried food. It is always best to check the label for the date of manufacture. Most dates on Japanese products do not follow the Gregorian calendar. Rather, they use a system whereby they count the year of the reign of the Emperor. Emperor Hirohito is an elderly man, and 1988 is the sixty-third year of his reign, which is known as Shōwa (the era of "Bright Peace"). Dates often appear on packages as serial numbers; a product manufactured on April 1, 1988, would be labeled 4163 or 4.1.63.

ABURA AGÉ (fried bean curd). An inexpensive, highly nutritious, and versatile food, *abura agé* finds its way into many Japanese dishes. (In this book there is a recipe calling for fried bean curd as an ingredient in a soup.) Fried bean curd should be kept refrigerated at all times and should be consumed within 3 days of purchase. Freezing changes the texture of the product, making it unpleasantly spongy, and I do not recommend it, although you will find fried bean curd imported from Japan in the freezer section of your Oriental market. Buy locally made bean curd products whenever possible. Fried bean curd needs to be blanched just before using, to remove the thin film of oil that covers the packaged slices.

AKA MISO. See *miso*.

AMAZU SHŌGA (pink pickled ginger). This mild but sprightly ginger condiment is usually served as a palate cleanser at a *sushi* bar. It is an ingredient in several *sushi* recipes in this book, but could be served alongside any *sushi* dish.

Amazu shōga is sold in glass jars or hermetically sealed plastic tubs and bags. It does not have to be refrigerated until the package has been opened. Most often, the pink pickled ginger is broadly and thinly sliced, but sometimes it is cut in julienne strips. Some brands are more intensely pink than others; the natural color is a very pale peach or yellow. Almost all brands contain some food coloring to heighten the natural blush shade that results from the chemical interaction between fresh, very young ginger shoots and rice vinegar. Pickled ginger will keep, covered and refrigerated, for many months.

AO NORI (sea herb flakes). This is one of many sea vegetables and herbs the Japanese enjoy. This particular alga is harvested from shallow ocean beds; then it is dried and packaged in glass jars, alone or combined with other terrestrial herbs and spices. I've called for sea herb flakes as a garnish in a few rice recipes where their fresh seashore aroma encourages hearty appetites.

Store your bottle of sea herb flakes on a dry shelf, away from direct sunlight and heat. They will not spoil, but their delicate sea-air aroma fades after several months. The full aromatic power of the herb can best be brought out by rubbing it between your fingertips or the palms of your hands just before using it.

BAINIKU (pickled plum paste). See *umé-boshi*.

BEAN PASTE. See *miso*.

BENI SHŌGA (red pickled ginger). This is a sharp, lively ginger pickle that is served as a garnish or condiment with many Japanese dishes. In this book I've called for it in a few fresh fish and *sushi* recipes.

Red pickled ginger is usually sold whole, sliced, or julienned, in glass jars or sealed plastic tubs. *Beni* is a natural dye known from ancient days, when it was used for cosmetic as well as culinary purposes. (*Kuchi beni* means "lipstick" in

Japanese; *kuchi* is "mouth" and *beni* is "red.") Be careful when you use red pickled ginger; it can stain plates and cutting boards. It's best to lay the ginger on paper towels first to blot up excess colored liquid.

Once you have opened your package, store it in the refrigerator, where it will keep, covered and in its original liquid, for many months. Drain just before serving.

CHIKUWA (roasted seafood sausage). A forcemeat of white-fleshed fishes (mainly pollack) is seasoned and molded around bamboo sticks before being roasted over a fire. The sausage is then slipped from the stick, leaving a hole through the length of it. Many kinds of commercially prepared *chikuwa* (literally "circling bamboo") are available in the refrigerator and freezer cases of Oriental groceries. Kibun brand, which packages five sticks in a cellophane wrapper, is usually a good choice. Refrigerate and use within 5 days of purchase.

DAIKON (Japanese white radish). This white root is extremely versatile; it can be grated or shredded and eaten raw, it can be steamed or braised and sauced or included in stews, and it can be pickled or dried. I've called for grated or shredded *daikon* in a number of recipes where the crunch and crisp, sharp flavor make a welcome contrast to the seafood preparation.

When shopping, choose *daikon* with a luminous quality to the unbroken skin and a firm, dense, and hefty feel in the hand. If you can find roots with their leaves still attached, all the better. Store the radish uncovered in the vegetable bin of your refrigerator. It will stay crisp (best for grating and shredding for salads) for 2–3 days.

DASHI (basic sea stock). This subtle sea broth has always been essential to the traditional cooking of Japan and continues to play an importaqnt role in even the most modern and Westernized kitchens. Made from *kombu* (kelp) and

katsuo bushi (dried bonito flakes), it imparts a delicate smoky sea nuance to all foods cooked in it.

DASHI KOMBU. See *kombu.*

ENOKIDAKÉ (slender creamy white mushrooms). These delicate fungi have an almost floral aroma and are used by the Japanese in soups and braised dishes. The Japanese never eat them raw, although they cook them only briefly (usually a matter of seconds; at most 2 or 3 minutes).

Enoki, as they are being called in the United States (the *také* or *daké,* by the way, means "fungi," are grown in California nearly year-round. They come packaged in 100-gram (3½-ounce) clumps in sealed cellophane bags. The bottom of the bag is opaque, hiding the unattractive, but entirely normal, moldy growth of the stems. Peek through the cellophane and examine the small knob-like caps at the end of the slender stalks; they should appear dry. If they look damp or slimy, the mushrooms are well past their prime.

After buying *enoki,* refrigerate them. They should stay fresh for 5–6 days, although that depends upon the age of the mushrooms when you purchased them. Just before using the mushrooms, rinse them under cold water, shake off excess moisture, and trim and discard the bottom half.

GINGER. Fresh ginger is very different from the dried, pickled, or powdered forms. Pale gold shiny-skinned knobs of fresh ginger grown in Hawaii are now increasingly available in supermarkets throughout the continental United States. Choose firm knobs; break off a piece to check the aroma. You will often notice a bluish rim on the inner edge of fresh ginger; that is fine and typical of certain botanical types. Ginger tends to be stringy, and you'll find that I often recommend that you squeeze the gratings to extract the juice. A Japanese grater, called an *oroshi-gané,* with its well to catch the gratings and juice, is a convenient tool to have.

GOMA (sesame seeds). See sesame seeds.

GOMA ABURA (aromatic sesame oil). This dark, nut-flavored vegetable oil is best used to add aroma to other oils. Dark sesame oil cannot be used by itself for deep-frying. (There is a type of cold-pressed sesame oil processed from white seeds that can resist the high temperatures of a deep-fryer, but it is very expensive and difficult to find here in the United States.) A few drops of the dark oil will nicely flavor other cooking oils. Buy just a small bottle of the deep-amber-colored oil unless you plan on using a great deal of it within 2 or 3 months. Store the oil on a cool, dry shelf in your cupboard.

HAKUSAI (Chinese cabbage). This leafy pale cabbage is popular throughout the Orient. Its English name shows that its popularity in the West stems from its use in Chinese cooking. The *hakusai* grown and harvested in America is sweeter than its Japanese counterpart and quite delicious raw in salads.

When buying Chinese cabbage, look for compact heads that feel fairly heavy. Ribs should be a pearly white (though speckling on the outer ribs is quite common) and leaves a pale to medium shade of green. Most produce markets will cut a large head in half or into quarters for you if you need less than the average 2-pound head. Store Chinese cabbage wrapped in a clean kitchen towel in the vegetable bin of your refrigerator. It will stay fresh for about 1 week.

HARUSAMÉ (cellophane noodles). Literally translated, *harusamé* means "spring rain." This poetic name refers to the transparent, almost glassy, quality of the softened noodles.

Harusamé are found packaged in a variety of ways in Oriental groceries. Chinese packages often refer to them as *saifun,* or bean-thread noodles, made from the starch of mung beans. The Chinese product is typically packed in skeins of crinkly noodles held together with rubber bands and covered with cellophane wrap. The Japanese packages have straighter, thicker strands, packed in an orderly fashion in a clear

cellophane bag; the label often says "bean starch noodles," or occasionally "potato starch noodles." Either kind is fine. These and other noodle products should be stored in an airtight container on a dark shelf.

HIJIKI (black sea vegetable). This dried sea vegetable, which looks like black threads, is sold in cellophane bags. I prefer to buy the shorter lengths called *mei hijiki* or "*hijiki* buds" whenever possible. They tend to be more uniform in shape and more tender. When soaking *hijiki* before cooking it, place it in a large bowl because it will expand to nearly 10 times its volume. Store any unused portion of dried *hijiki* in a canister or other closed container away from heat and light. *Hijiki* has a shelf life of several years if stored properly.

ICHIMI TŌGARASHI (powdered red chili pepper). This product contains only hot chili peppers, hence its name *ichi* ("one") and *mi* ("flavor"). Do not confuse it with a similar product called *shichimi,* or "seven flavors." *Ichimi tōgarashi* is sold in small tins and glass jars. Store it as you would salt or pepper.

IKURA (red salmon caviar). This is the most prized of the red caviars in Japan. Red is a color of felicity, and these large glossy globes are often served on happy occasions. Price is usually a good indication of quality. Each of the eggs should be nearly ¼ inch in diameter and full (no puckering), the color a vivid orangy red. Store fresh caviar in the refrigerator, covered, for up to a week.

KAIWARÉ. See radish sprouts.

KAMPYŌ (dried gourd ribbons). Large pale pumpkin-like gourds called *fukube* are harvested and peeled into long ½-inch-wide ribbons and dried for several days. These are sold in cellophane bags containing very long (several-yard) lengths or short (6-inch) lengths. It is best to buy the uncut gourd ribbons since they are easier to use when tying up

edible packages such as the Golden Purse *Sushi* on page 72.

Refrigerate what you don't use after opening. Stored in a closed plastic bag, the dried gourd (which is still pliable, not brittle) will keep for months.

KANTEN (agar-agar). This gelatin is processed from sea vegetation, specifically a plant called *tengusa* ("heavenly grass"). The jelling property of this plant, particularly after it has been freeze-dried, is quite remarkable (it will solidify liquid without refrigeration) and has been known and used in the Orient for many centuries.

Kanten is usually sold as two sticks of what appear to be brittle cellophane wrapped in what really is thin cellophane. One stick can usually jell about 1¾ cups liquid. Agar-agar also comes in flakes; 1 tablespoon jells 1 cup of liquid. More recently, powdered *kanten* has come on the market; one packet of powder jells about 1⅔ cups liquid. A great deal depends upon the chemistry of the specific liquid used.

Store *kanten* in an airtight container on your shelf; it will keep, dried, indefinitely.

KARASHI (hot Japanese mustard). The Japanese favor a sharp, bright yellow mustard that is easily made from a powder. S&B brand hot mustard is usually a good choice. Store the powder in its original tin, with the lid closed, on a shelf away from light, heat, and moisture.

KASU (lees). *Saké* wine is made from fermenting rice, and the lees, or leftover fermented rice grains, are often used to pickle fish and vegetables. You'll find pressed sheets of *kasu* in cellophane packages in the refrigerated section of your Oriental grocery. *Kasu* has a refrigerated shelf life of several months.

KATSUO BUSHI (dried bonito flakes). A tuna-like fish called bonito or bonita in English and *katsuo* in Japanese is found in fairly temperate waters. The best-known area of Japan is

Tosa, on the Pacific coast of the island of Shikoku. Fresh bonito is an early summer delicacy in Japan; year-round the dried fillets are flaked and used to make stocks and sauces.

Most packages of dried fish flakes combine bonito with other less expensive fishes such as mackerel and sardines. The price will tell you. Traditionally, every kitchen kept whole dried fillets, which were then rubbed over a sharp blade attached to a wooden box. A drawer in the box fills with shavings, which can easily be removed. Just as freshly ground coffee beans are far superior to beans ground weeks before, so freshly shaved bonito is far superior to preshaved flakes. Today, though, it is hard to find these boxes or people who use them. Instead, it is more common to see scissors cutting open 5-gram packets of preshaved flakes. If you will be using *katsuo bushi* only occasionally, it is best to buy these small packets, affectionately labeled "fresh pack." Five or six of these packets are sold as a unit in either a cardboard box or a large plastic bag. Large bags of flakes go rancid rather quickly once opened.

KOMBU (kelp). The natural taste-enhancing properties of *Laminaria japonica* and *Laminaria ochotensis*, two of many commonly used sea vegetables in Japan, have been known for centuries. These sturdy kelps are used primarily for stock making, though they are also cooked and eaten as vegetables.

When shopping, ask for *dashi kombu* ("kelp for stock making") and let price be your guide; the superior product is more expensive. The whitish, chalky-like powder is not an indication of mold or spoilage. The color and thickness of kelp can vary from thick and stony gray to thin and green with a reddish cast. All kelp should be stored in an airtight container on a dark shelf, where it will keep indefinitely.

MIRIN (syrupy rice wine). With only an 8 percent alcohol content, *mirin* is often sold in ordinary supermarkets. It is not a drinking wine. Instead, it is used as a seasoning and glazing agent in cooking other foods.

Store your bottle on a dark, dry shelf. The cap and rim should be wiped well after each use, or else they will stick badly, as do caps on bottles of maple and other syrups.

MISO (fermented bean paste). There are hundreds, if not thousands, of types of *miso* that the Japanese enjoy regularly. Whether mild or pungent, they are all made from the fermentation of soybeans. Fermented bean paste is used to thicken and season soups, to make marinades and sauces, and as a seasoning in fish and shellfish pastes or forcemeats.

Generally, *miso* falls into two types, dark and light, though there are medium shades (and flavors), too. For the recipes calling for dark bean paste you could use any kind of *aka* (literally "red") *miso*, though I recommend *Sendai miso*, a regional type. Similarly, for any light bean paste I recommend *Saikyo miso*, though any *shiro* (literally "white") *miso* will do.

After opening the plastic package or tub, reseal and store it in the refrigerator for up to 2 months for optimal aroma, though spoilage is rare even after 6 months or more. A white and/or green moldy growth around the edges or across the surface of the bean paste is a sign of unwanted bacteria. Scrape off the mold and use the remaining bean paste within a day or two.

MITSUBA (trefoil). A three-leafed slender-stalked herb with a subtle fresh flavor, *mitsuba* is occasionally available fresh in the spring and fall. Ideally the stalks will curve slightly and be a pale green; the leaves should be no larger than 1 inch across and a darker, more vibrant shade of green. Avoid yellowed or brown-edged leaves and limp stalks. It is best to select a bunch that still has its roots attached and to trim them off only as needed. The leaves and stems are edible. Wrap *mitsuba* in paper towels that have been moistened with a drop or two of water, and store it in the vegetable bin of your refrigerator. It should keep well for 5–6 days.

NERI MISO (seasoned fermented bean paste). A mixture of fermented bean paste (*miso*), sugar, and rice wine, stirred and

cooked together, *neri miso* can be made with either light or dark bean pastes.

NERI UMÉ (pickled plum paste). See *umé-boshi.*

NERI UNI (sea urchin paste). See *uni.*

NOODLES. See *harusamé* (cellophane noodles), *soba* (buckwheat noodles).

NORI (seaweed). This is a generic term for a variety of marine vegetables cultivated and harvested in Japan. It is unfortunate that the derogatory word "weed" has come into such common usage. The Japanese have cultivated and harvested sea vegetables for centuries, and among the many varieties regularly consumed in Japan, *Asakusa nori*—paper-thin sheets of pressed, dried alga—is the most popular here in the United States. Throughout this book I recommend the purchase of *yaki nori,* which is high-quality *Akasusa nori* that has been pretoasted. It is best to buy flat, unfolded, full-sized (about 7½ x 6½-inch) sheets of pretoasted seaweed. These come in ten- and fifty-sheet packages. After opening the pack, store them, with their anti-moisture packets from the original package, in a closed bag or tin, in the freezer. The sheets will defrost instantaneously and may be refrozen any number of times.

OKOMÉ (raw rice). The Japanese typically eat a short-grained rice that has been hulled, washed, and then boiled in unseasoned water. Rice is important to the Japanese, and they have many words for it. *Gohan* means "cooked rice" or "meal"; *okomé* means "uncooked rice." The hulls of processed rice are crushed into a powder called *nuka,* which is used to pickle and preserve certain foods. The word for unhulled rice is *gen mai.* the Japanese also steam hulled, glutinous rice called *mochi-gomé* to make various dishes, most famous of which is the rice taffy known as *omochi.*

California is now growing excellent Japanese-style short-grained rice, which is being marketed throughout the United

States under a number of different labels. Most stores sell 2- and 5-pound packages in addition to the 25-pound bags bought by most Japanese households. Transfer your rice from the original paper bag to an airtight container, and store it on a cool, dry, dark shelf. It will keep well for at least 1 year.

Recently *shin mai*, or newly harvested rice, has been available in the fall. Storage procedures are the same for all varieties of raw rice, but cooking varies; see page 213 for information on cooking rice.

PANKO (Japanese coarse bread crumbs). The Japanese first learned to make bread from the Portuguese and adapted their word for it, *pão*. In Japanese *ko* means "flour," "crumb," or "powder." Japanese *panko* have pointed, irregular shapes, which makes for an unusually crunchy surface when deep-fried. There are several brands and varieties available; all are sold in clear plastic bags. I prefer those that have no egg or honey in the ingredients. Store *panko* in an airtight container on a dark dry shelf for up to 6 months.

PLUM PASTE. See *umé-boshi*.

RADISH SPROUTS. This deliciously sharp, fresh sprout looks pretty on any platter and can liven up an otherwise bland green salad. In Japan they are known as *kaiwaré* (which means "split seashell"—the cleft, clover-like leaf reminds the Japanese of an open seashell) or *tsumamina* (*tsumamu* means "to pinch" or "pluck" and the suffix *na* refers to edible greens). These nutritious and delicious sprouts are highly perishable and should be eaten within a day or two of purchase. Look for intensely green leaves (yellowing is a sign of age), and crisp, clean, pale stalks with the roots still attached. Store them loosely wrapped in slightly damp paper towels in the vegetable bin of your refrigerator.

RICE. See *okomé*.

SAKÉ (Japanese rice wine). This is a generic name for the alcoholic beverage distilled from steamed rice. It is also known as *nihon shu* ("Japanese wine"). There are two types of rice wine: *kara kuchi,* or dry, and *ama kuchi,* or sweet. The choice for drinking depends upon your personal taste. For cooking purposes, any type or brand of drinking *saké* will do as long as the label does not say "cooking wine," which usually indicates a mixture of inferior rice wines and occasionally the addition of sugar or other additives. Price is a good indication of quality. Store it, tightly capped, on a dark kitchen shelf.

SANSHO (Japanese pepper). The berry of the prickly ash plant is dried and crushed into a delicate and highly aromatic powder that is called *sansho* or *kona-zansho.* It is sold in small jars or plastic containers, and once opened should be stored in the freezer to protect its delicate scent. Occasionally whole *sansho* berries that have been salted and partially dried are available in clear plastic bags. These are wonderful to add to simmered fish or seafood dishes. Store the berries in a closed container in the freezer.

SEA VEGETABLES. See *ao nori* (sea herb flakes), *hijiki* (black threads), *kombu* (kelp), *wakamé* (sea tangle), and *yaki nori* (paper-thin sheets).

SESAME SEEDS. There are two kinds of sesame seeds used in Japanese cooking: white and black. White sesame (*shiro goma*) comes to market in two forms, hulled and unhulled. The unhulled seeds are a beige color and tend to have a nuttier flavor than the hulled ones. The smooth, cream-colored hulled seeds crush more easily to make a rich paste. Black sesame (*kuro goma*) has medicinal uses (in salves and ointments for the skin) as well as culinary ones in Japan. It is the black seeds from which dark aromatic sesame oil is pressed.

Never purchase preroasted sesame seeds. Always dry-roast the seeds yourself just before using them. Once they have

been roasted, the oils come to the surface (that is what makes them so wonderfully aromatic!) and can go rancid quickly thereafter. Store sesame seeds in a closed container on a dry, cool shelf in your cupboard.

SHARI (seasoned rice for *sushi*). A word used mainly in *sushi* bars.

SHICHIMI TŌGARASHI (seven-spice powder). The Japanese use dried chili peppers, usually in powdered form, to season several dishes. Here the fiery powdered pods have been blended with six other herbs and spices (black and white sesame, green laver, dried citron peel, rape seed, and *sansho* pepper). This mixture is sold in small glass jars; store it, tightly capped, on a dark, dry shelf.

SHIITAKÉ (dark oak mushrooms). Fresh *shiitaké* have large bark-colored caps which, depending upon the variety, are smooth or nubbly with lighter-colored striations. A peek under the ''umbrella'' of either type reveals white webbing. Both kinds of *shiitaké* are grown in Virginia and are delicious. The average size of the cap is 1½ inches across, with 1-inch white stems. The Japanese do not eat uncooked *shiitaké*, though they cook them only briefly. The fresh fungi should be aromatic and plump; residual dirt clinging to caps or stems is irrelevant. Store the fresh fungi in an open plastic bag in your vegetable bin for up to 5 days.

Dried *shiitaké* are available imported from many Asian countries. Price is an indication of quality; the nubbly thick-capped *donko* variety is the most prized. Store dried fungi on a dark shelf in an airtight container with the anti-moisture packet from the original cellophane bag.

SHIRO MISO. See *miso*.

SHISO (broad flat Japanese herb). A distant botanical relative of mint, *shiso* goes by several names in English and Japanese. ''Beefsteak-plant leaf'' is one English name, ''herb leaf''

another. In addition to *shiso*, in Japanese the leaves are also called *ōba*, meaning "big leaf." Traditionally a summer herb, it is cultivated year-round in the United States, though the summer months still yield the tastiest leaves. *Shiso* is typically sold in Styrofoam plates covered with clear plastic wrap, each packet containing ten leaves. Keep it refrigerated at home, wrapped in damp paper towels and clear plastic wrap. The broad-leafed herb will stay fresh for 5–6 days. The first sign of spoilage is the appearance of dark areas on leaves or stems.

SOBA (buckwheat noodles). Packages of dried buckwheat noodles are available at all Oriental groceries, and at many supermarkets too. Sometimes a grated yam called *yama imo* has been added as a binder to the dough before the noodles are rolled and cut, but this does not affect the taste of the noodle. Store as you would any dried pasta product.

SOY SAUCE. There are many different types of soy sauce available, each for a slightly different purpose, but for most dishes you will find regular soy, or what the Japanese call *koikuchi shōyu,* suitable. I find the smaller-sized tins the most convenient package for my home, but we do use quite a bit of soy sauce. For those who use it only occasionally, the smaller unbreakable clear bottles are best. Although soy sauce does not spoil, its subtle, full-bodied bean aroma does fade after several months. Keep opened bottles tightly capped on a dark shelf in your kitchen.

The different labels on soy sauces can be confusing. The light-colored but intensely flavored *usukuchi shōyu* has its own entry in this glossary. The very dark *tamari* soy sauce is mainly used for fish *sashimi* (fresh slices of uncooked fish). The word *tamari* means "filled up" or "accumulated" and refers to the thicker sauce that accumulates at the bottom of large vats of soy sauce. Health food stores will often sell *tamari* soy sauce as a nutritionally richer sauce than ordinary soy. It is a generally more intense sauce, with a higher ratio of minerals, including sodium.

The newer reduced-sodium soy sauces have been devel-

oped in response to the American consumer. I feel they are of limited use and questionable flavor; I would prefer to choose recipes that use little or no soy sauce, or to dilute regular soy sauce with basic sea stock and/or rice wine, to achieve a reduced sodium content. Read the labels carefully, and calculate your own dietary needs.

SU (rice vinegar). This mild but fragrant vinegar is used in many Japanese dishes. Many Americans become instant fans of its subtle verve and never return to harsh distilled white vinegar. Several brands are regularly available, and each company puts out several kinds of vinegar, so read the labels carefully. The most expensive, and the absolute best, is pure *komé-zu*: rice vinegar that is the first pressing from the fermented rice. Ordinary rice vinegar is made fron successive pressings. Seasoned rice vinegar for making *sushi* has sugar, salt, and sometimes MSG added to it (see *sushi su*, below). Store your vinegar tightly capped on a dark, dry shelf in the kitchen. The vinegar will darken slightly with age and with exposure to light or heat. .

SUSHI (vinegared rice). There is a tremendous variety of vinegared rice dishes, collectively known as *sushi*. See pages 49–85 for recipes.

SUSHI SU (seasoned rice vinegar). Examine all writing on the package carefully to determine if the product labeled "rice vinegar" is this preparation, which is meant for making *sushi*, or an unseasoned vinegar, which would have to be seasoned with sugar and salt before it is used for *sushi*.

TŌFU (bean curd). Dried soybeans are crushed and boiled, and the snowy liquid that results is solidified into pudding-like loaves that are usually referred to in English as "bean curd" cakes or blocks. Depending upon such variables as coagulating agent, lining and type of molds, time, and pressure, a number of rather different-looking products result:
  Kinugoshi ("silk-strained") bean curd is very soft, delicate,

and smooth. It is fragile like custard and when freshly made, has a delightfully nutty aftertaste.

Momen ("cotton-wrapped") bean curd is firmer and more roughly textured throughout, with a noticeable crosshatch design on the surface; this is from the weave of the *sarashi* cloth that lined the molds. This kind of bean curd is meatier than the "silky" variety.

Pressed *tōfu* are usually smaller, pillow-shaped loaves of dense "cotton-wrapped" bean curd. They are more common in Chinese and Korean markets than they are in Japanese ones, but they are fine for most dishes and especially good for floating in soups.

All types of bean curd are highly perishable and should be refrigerated, submerged in fresh water, for no more than 2 days. Cloudy water or a thin sticky film on the bean curd indicates spoilage; so does an off odor. Do not freeze *tōfu;* its texture becomes unpleasantly spongy.

TŌGARASHI (red chili peppers). The Japanese dry pepper pods and use them to spice up a number of dishes. The seeds are incendiary and should be avoided unless you have a mouth lined with asbestos. After handling the dried pepper pods, be sure to wash your hands; the natural oils can be particularly irritating.

TONKATSU SŌSU (dark, spicy sauce). The Japanese created this thick, aromatic sauce to complement their deep-fried breaded pork cutlets, called *tonkatsu.* The sauce is made from fruits (such as apples) and vegetables (such as tomatoes) and is also delicious served with fried shrimp and chicken. Bottles of *tonkatsu sōsu* can be found at any Oriental grocery; store as you would ketchup.

UMÉ-BOSHI (pickled plums). These dusty pink wrinkled spheres seem innocuous enough sitting in their clear plastic tubs on the shelf of a Japanese grocery store. In reality they possess the most explosively refreshing, mouth-puckering taste imaginable! Many Japanese wake up to pickled plums

with their breakfast bowl of rice, just as Americans rely on a strong cup of coffee to get them going first thing in the morning. Pickled plums are also thought to settle and cure intestinal problems. In this cookbook I've called for the pulp (*bainiku* or *neri umé*) of pickled plums to perk up a sauce and a salad dressing. Either make your own paste by mashing moist, softly wrinkled large plums, or buy the paste in a clear plastic tube or tub. Cover and refrigerate the plums and/or paste after opening; either will stay fresh for at least a year.

UNI (sea urchin). These spiked sea creatures look like chestnuts. The soft, briny-tasting gonads are the edible portion. Usually a gold or reddish gold in color, fresh *uni* is a costly delicacy in Japan. Here the price is usually fairly reasonable. Have your fish market cut open the spiked creature and remove the roe, or purchase already removed roe from a Japanese food store. Use *uni* within 24 hours and keep it refrigerated until you use it.

A paste called *neri uni* is also sold, bottled, at most Oriental groceries. This briny paste is used as a seasoning for other ingredients; in this book I call for *neri uni* to be mixed with egg yolks to make a glaze for broiled fish.

USUKUCHI SHŌYU (light soy sauce). This soy sauce is lighter in color but saltier than ordinary *shōyu*, or soy sauce. It is favored in the southern and southwestern regions of Japan, where they feel the deeper color of soy stains and muddies the appearance of the food. The natives of the northern and northeastern regions favor the deep reddish-brown tones of foods cooked in regular soy sauce and think *usukuchi shōyu* an insipid, pallid seasoning. Obviously there is strong regional prejudice at work here! For most recipes, regular soy sauce is fine (I spend most of my time in Tokyo), though for some, the paler, more delicate amber of light soy sauce is better (my husband's family comes from the south).

Read the labels carefully; the reduced-salt varieties are not necessarily light in color, and the paler soy sauces are not necessarily lower in sodium.

WAKAMÉ (sea-tangle). Fresh *wakamé* is harvested in the spring and dried to use throughout the year. Dried *wakamé* must be soaked in cold water for 10–15 minutes before being used in soups or salads. Dried *wakamé* is packaged in cellophane bags; look for lightweight, dark green, almost-black tangles. Store in a cupboard away from light, heat, and moisture.

WASABI (Japanese horseradish). This delightfully hot spice is used to highlight many *sushi, sashimi,* and cooked fish dishes. The *wasabi* root is rather nubby and usually grows between 3 and 5 inches in length. Fresh roots are hard to find, but if your local Japanese food store has them in their refrigerated case, by all means treat yourself—you'll find herbaceous aroma as well as fire. Choose pale green roots with even coloration and darker ruffly leaves. Dark speckling on the root can be an early sign of spoilage; but look carefully—sometimes it's just earth clinging to it. Whittle away the leaves and stem and grate just as much of the root as you need. Cover the rest with clear plastic wrap and refrigerate. The roots should keep well for at least a week.

Most often *wasabi* is sold as a powder, in tins, or as a paste in tubes. The powdered form is preferable. Buy a small tin unless you use a great deal of the stuff; although the powder does not spoil, it often develops a dusty, stale aftertaste within a few months of opening. Recap the can tightly after each use and store the tin on a dark, dry shelf in your cupboard.

YAKI NORI (toasted paper-thin seaweed). Small aquatic plants (called *nori,* in Japanese) are harvested, rinsed, chopped, and mashed into a paste that is then spread across bamboo mats and dried. This produces rectangular sheets of seaweed, also called *nori,* about 7 x 8 inches in size. Toasting the sheets improves the flavor of the seaweed. The generic name for already toasted sheets of seaweed is *yaki nori.*

Some packages may be labeled *yaki-zushi nori* because these dark, crisp sheets are used primarily at the *sushi* bar. Some of these sheets are precut into strips.

If you find a package labeled *Asakusa nori,* it will contain untoasted sheets of seaweed. The name *Asakusa* refers to the area in Tokyo where most *nori* production used to be.

If you find a package labeled *aji-tsuké nori,* that means the seaweed has been seasoned with soy sauce (and MSG, too, in most cases).

I recommend that you purchase unseasoned, pretoasted, uncut sheets of seaweed.

YUZU (Japanese citron). This wonderfully aromatic fruit is green in the autumn, turning yellow in the winter. Only the peel is eaten in Japan, where *yuzu* adds a nuance of flavor to soups, sauces, and salads. *Yuzu* essence, extracted from pressed peel, can be either a clear, colorless liquid or an opaque, yellowish one. The essence is sometimes sold pre-mixed with vegetable oil to make *yuzu abura,* a fragrant salad oil. All of these products come bottled and are sold in many Oriental groceries. Refrigerate after opening.

A Word of Caution About Pollution and Parasites

L ike all foods, fish and seafood can be adversely affected by man-made pollutants, such as PCBs, and by naturally occurring toxins, such as "red tide." Local fish and wildlife officials in conjunction with local departments of health monitor the commercial catches of finfish and shellfish. When problems do occur, they are widely publicized by the media, and affected species are not found at the marketplace. Seafood purchased through reputable commercial sources, therefore, presents no problems. Those who want to eat fish or shellfish caught on their own should check with local authorities.

On rare occasions, a condition known as "red tide" occurs, when an excessive accumulation of a toxic reddish brown plankton forms on the surface of the water. Filter-feeders such as clams, oysters, and particularly mussels consume large quantities of the plankton, and although they remain unharmed by the toxins they consume, humans become very ill when they eat affected bivalves. Cooking does not destroy the toxins.

Certain species of fish are more affected than others by chemical pollutants. In general, fatty fishes such as tuna, striped bass, eel, and bluefish are the most readily affected. Cooking, marinating, and freezing do not eliminate the danger.

 **257**

Several varieties of parasites also are of concern, especially when fish is eaten uncooked. Parasites—worms—affect certain species more than others. In general freshwater fish, such as trout and carp, and fish that spend part of their life cycle in fresh water, such as salmon, are most prone to worms that cause severe illness when ingested by human beings. Cooking kills the parasites that cause gastrointestinal illness. Commercial freezing, at minus 40 degrees for 15 hours or more, will also kill all parasites.

Index

Index

Index

Index

Index

 265

Index

 267

Index

Index